Think Data Structures
Algorithms and Information Retrieval in Java

Allen B. Downey

Beijing · Boston · Farnham · Sebastopol · Tokyo

Think Data Structures

by Allen B. Downey

Published by O'Reilly Media, Inc., 1005 Gravenstein Highway North, Sebastopol, CA 95472.

O'Reilly books may be purchased for educational, business, or sales promotional use. Online editions are also available for most titles (*http://oreilly.com/safari*). For more information, contact our corporate/institutional sales department: 800-998-9938 or *corporate@oreilly.com*.

Editors: Nan Barber and Brian Foster
Production Editor: Kristen Brown
Copyeditor: Charles Roumeliotis
Proofreader: Amanda Kersey

Indexer: Allen B. Downey
Interior Designer: David Futato
Cover Designer: Karen Montgomery
Illustrator: Rebecca Demarest

July 2017:   First Edition

Revision History for the First Edition

2017-07-07:   First Release

978-1-491-97239-7

[LSI]

Table of Contents

Preface

The Philosophy Behind the Book

Data structures and algorithms are among the most important inventions of the last 50 years, and they are fundamental tools software engineers need to know. But in my opinion, most of the books on these topics are too theoretical, too big, and too "bottom up":

Too theoretical
> Mathematical analysis of algorithms is based on simplifying assumptions that limit its usefulness in practice. Many presentations of this topic gloss over the simplifications and focus on the math. In this book I present the most practical subset of this material and omit or de-emphasize the rest.

Too big
> Most books on these topics are at least 500 pages, and some are more than 1,000. By focusing on the topics I think are most useful for software engineers, I kept this book under 150 pages.

Too "bottom up"
> Many data structures books focus on how data structures work (the implementations), with less about how to use them (the interfaces). In this book, I go "top down", starting with the interfaces. Readers learn to use the structures in the Java Collections Framework before getting into the details of how they work.

Finally, some books present this material out of context and without motivation: it's just one damn data structure after another! I try to liven it up by organizing the topics around an application—web search—that uses data structures extensively, and is an interesting and important topic in its own right.

This application motivates some topics that are not usually covered in an introductory data structures class, including persistent data structures with Redis.

I have made difficult decisions about what to leave out, but I have made some compromises. I include a few topics that most readers will never use, but that they might be expected to know, possibly in a technical interview. For these topics, I present both the conventional wisdom as well as my reasons to be skeptical.

This book also presents basic aspects of software engineering practice, including version control and unit testing. Most chapters include an exercise that allows readers to apply what they have learned. Each exercise provides automated tests that check the solution. And for most exercises, I present my solution at the beginning of the next chapter.

Prerequisites

This book is intended for college students in computer science and related fields, as well as professional software engineers, people training in software engineering, and people preparing for technical interviews.

Before you start this book, you should know Java pretty well; in particular, you should know how to define a new class that extends an existing class or implements an inter face. If your Java is rusty, here are two books you might start with:

- Downey and Mayfield, *Think Java* (O'Reilly Media, 2016), which is intended for people who have never programmed before
- Sierra and Bates, *Head First Java* (O'Reilly Media, 2005), which is appropriate for people who already know another programming language

If you are not familiar with interfaces in Java, you might want to work through the tutorial called "What Is an Interface?" at *http://thinkdast.com/interface*.

One vocabulary note: the word "interface" can be confusing. In the context of an **application programming interface** (API), it refers to a set of classes and methods that provide certain capabilities.

In the context of Java, it also refers to a language feature, similar to a class, that specifies a set of methods. To help avoid confusion, I'll use "interface" in the normal typeface for the general idea of an interface, and interface in the code typeface for the Java language feature.

You should also be familiar with type parameters and generic types. For example, you should know how create an object with a type parameter, like ArrayList<Integer>. If not, you can read about type parameters at *http://thinkdast.com/types*.

You should be familiar with the Java Collections Framework (JCF), which you can read about at *http://thinkdast.com/collections*. In particular, you should know about the List interface and the classes ArrayList and LinkedList.

Ideally you should be familiar with Apache Ant, which is an automated build tool for Java. You can read more about Ant at *http://thinkdast.com/anttut*.

And you should be familiar with JUnit, which is a unit testing framework for Java. You can read more about it at *http://thinkdast.com/junit*.

Working with the Code

The code for this book is in a Git repository at *http://thinkdast.com/repo*.

Git is a **version control system** that allows you to keep track of the files that make up a project. A collection of files under Git's control is called a **repository**.

GitHub is a hosting service that provides storage for Git repositories and a convenient web interface. It provides several ways to work with the code:

- You can create a copy of the repository on GitHub by pressing the Fork button. If you don't already have a GitHub account, you'll need to create one. After forking, you'll have your own repository on GitHub that you can use to keep track of code you write. Then you can **clone** the repository, which downloads a copy of the files to your computer.

- Alternatively, you could clone the repository without forking. If you choose this option, you don't need a GitHub account, but you won't be able to save your changes on GitHub.

- If you don't want to use Git at all, you can download the code in a ZIP archive using the Download button on the GitHub page, or this link: *http://think dast.com/zip*.

After you clone the repository or unzip the ZIP file, you should have a directory called ThinkDataStructures with a subdirectory called code.

The examples in this book were developed and tested using Java SE Development Kit 7. If you are using an older version, some examples will not work. If you are using a more recent version, they should all work.

Conventions Used in This Book

The following typographical conventions are used in this book:

Italic
> Indicates emphasis, keystrokes, menu options, URLs, and email addresses.

Bold
> Used for new terms where they are defined.

`Constant width`

Used for program listings, as well as within paragraphs to refer to filenames, file extensions, and program elements such as variable and function names, data types, statements, and keywords.

`Constant width bold`

Shows commands or other text that should be typed literally by the user.

Safari® Books Online

 Safari Books Online (*www.safaribooksonline.com*) is an on-demand digital library that delivers expert content in both book and video form from the world's leading authors in technology and business.

Technology professionals, software developers, web designers, and business and creative professionals use Safari Books Online as their primary resource for research, problem solving, learning, and certification training.

Safari Books Online offers a range of plans and pricing for enterprise, government, education, and individuals.

Members have access to thousands of books, training videos, and prepublication manuscripts in one fully searchable database from publishers like O'Reilly Media, Prentice Hall Professional, Addison-Wesley Professional, Microsoft Press, Sams, Que, Peachpit Press, Focal Press, Cisco Press, John Wiley & Sons, Syngress, Morgan Kaufmann, IBM Redbooks, Packt, Adobe Press, FT Press, Apress, Manning, New Riders, McGraw-Hill, Jones & Bartlett, Course Technology, and hundreds more. For more information about Safari Books Online, please visit us online.

How to Contact Us

Please address comments and questions concerning this book to the publisher:

O'Reilly Media, Inc.
1005 Gravenstein Highway North
Sebastopol, CA 95472
800-998-9938 (in the United States or Canada)
707-829-0515 (international or local)
707-829-0104 (fax)

To comment or ask technical questions about this book, send email to *bookquestions@oreilly.com*.

For more information about our books, courses, conferences, and news, see our website at *http://www.oreilly.com*.

Find us on Facebook: *http://facebook.com/oreilly*

Follow us on Twitter: *http://twitter.com/oreillymedia*

Watch us on YouTube: *http://www.youtube.com/oreillymedia*

Contributors

This book is an adapted version of a curriculum I wrote for the Flatiron School in New York City, which offers a variety of online classes related to programming and web development. They offer a class based on this material, which provides an online development environment, help from instructors and other students, and a certificate of completion. You can find more information at *http://flatironschool.com*.

- At the Flatiron School, Joe Burgess, Ann John, and Charles Pletcher provided guidance, suggestions, and corrections from the initial specification all the way through implementation and testing. Thank you all!

- I am very grateful to my technical reviewers, Barry Whitman, Patrick White, and Chris Mayfield, who made many helpful suggestions and caught many errors. Of course, any remaining errors are my fault, not theirs!

- Thanks to the instructors and students in Data Structures and Algorithms at Olin College, who read this book and provided useful feedback.

- Charles Roumeliotis copyedited the book for O'Reilly Media and made many improvements.

If you have comments or ideas about the text, please send them to *feedback@greenteapress.com*.

CHAPTER 1

Interfaces

This book presents three topics:

Data structures
  Starting with the structures in the Java Collections Framework (JCF), you will learn how to use data structures like lists and maps, and you will see how they work.

Analysis of algorithms
  I present techniques for analyzing code and predicting how fast it will run and how much space (memory) it will require.

Information retrieval
  To motivate the first two topics, and to make the exercises more interesting, we will use data structures and algorithms to build a simple web search engine.

Here's an outline of the order of topics:

- We'll start with the List interface and you will write classes that implement this interface two different ways. Then we'll compare your implementations with the Java classes ArrayList and LinkedList.

- Next I'll introduce tree-shaped data structures and you will work on the first application: a program that reads pages from Wikipedia, parses the contents, and navigates the resulting tree to find links and other features. We'll use these tools to test the "Getting to Philosophy" conjecture (you can get a preview by reading *http://thinkdast.com/getphil*).

- We'll learn about the Map interface and Java's HashMap implementation. Then you'll write classes that implement this interface using a hash table and a binary search tree.

- Finally, you will use these classes (and a few others I'll present along the way) to implement a web search engine, including a crawler that finds and reads pages, an indexer that stores the contents of web pages in a form that can be searched efficiently, and a retriever that takes queries from a user and returns relevant results.

Let's get started.

Why Are There Two Kinds of List?

When people start working with the Java Collections Framework, they are sometimes confused about ArrayList and LinkedList. Why does Java provide two implementations of the List interface? And how should you choose which one to use? I will answer these questions in the next few chapters.

I'll start by reviewing interfaces and the classes that implement them, and I'll present the idea of "programming to an interface".

In the first few exercises, you'll implement classes similar to ArrayList and Linked List, so you'll know how they work, and we'll see that each of them has pros and cons. Some operations are faster or use less space with ArrayList; others are faster or smaller with LinkedList. Which one is better for a particular application depends on which operations it performs most often.

Interfaces in Java

A Java interface specifies a set of methods; any class that implements this interface has to provide these methods. For example, here is the source code for Comparable, which is an interface defined in the package java.lang:

```
public interface Comparable<T> {
    public int compareTo(T o);
}
```

This interface definition uses a type parameter, T, which makes Comparable a **generic type**. In order to implement this interface, a class has to

- Specify the type T refers to, and
- Provide a method named compareTo that takes an object as a parameter and returns an int.

For example, here's the source code for `java.lang.Integer`:

```
public final class Integer extends Number implements Comparable<Integer> {

    public int compareTo(Integer anotherInteger) {
        int thisVal = this.value;
        int anotherVal = anotherInteger.value;
        return (thisVal<anotherVal ? -1 : (thisVal==anotherVal ? 0 : 1));
    }

    // other methods omitted
}
```

This class extends `Number`, so it inherits the methods and instance variables of `Number`; and it implements `Comparable<Integer>`, so it provides a method named `compareTo` that takes an `Integer` and returns an `int`.

When a class declares that it implements an `interface`, the compiler checks that it provides all methods defined by the `interface`.

As an aside, this implementation of `compareTo` uses the "ternary operator", sometimes written ?:. If you are not familiar with it, you can read about it at *http://think dast.com/ternary*.

List Interface

The Java Collections Framework (JCF) defines an `interface` called `List` and provides two implementations, `ArrayList` and `LinkedList`.

The `interface` defines what it means to be a `List`; any class that implements this `interface` has to provide a particular set of methods, including `add`, `get`, `remove`, and about 20 more.

`ArrayList` and `LinkedList` provide these methods, so they can be used interchangeably. A method written to work with a `List` will work with an `ArrayList`, `LinkedList`, or any other object that implements `List`.

Here's a contrived example that demonstrates the point:

```
public class ListClientExample {
    private List list;

    public ListClientExample() {
        list = new LinkedList();
    }

    private List getList() {
        return list;
    }
```

```
    public static void main(String[] args) {
        ListClientExample lce = new ListClientExample();
        List list = lce.getList();
        System.out.println(list);
    }
}
```

ListClientExample doesn't do anything useful, but it has the essential elements of a class that **encapsulates** a List; that is, it contains a List as an instance variable. I'll use this class to make a point, and then you'll work with it in the first exercise.

The ListClientExample constructor initializes list by **instantiating** (that is, creating) a new LinkedList; the getter method called getList returns a reference to the internal List object; and main contains a few lines of code to test these methods.

The important thing about this example is that it uses List whenever possible and avoids specifying LinkedList or ArrayList unless it is necessary. For example, the instance variable is declared to be a List, and getList returns a List, but neither specifies which kind of list.

If you change your mind and decide to use an ArrayList, you only have to change the constructor; you don't have to make any other changes.

This style is called **interface-based programming**, or more casually, "programming to an interface" (see *http://thinkdast.com/interbaseprog*). Here we are talking about the general idea of an interface, not a Java interface.

When you use a library, your code should only depend on the interface, like List. It should not depend on a specific implementation, like ArrayList. That way, if the implementation changes in the future, the code that uses it will still work.

On the other hand, if the interface changes, the code that depends on it has to change, too. That's why library developers avoid changing interfaces unless absolutely necessary.

Exercise 1

Since this is the first exercise, we'll keep it simple. You will take the code from the previous section and **swap the implementation**; that is, you will replace the Linked List with an ArrayList. Because the code programs to an interface, you will be able to swap the implementation by changing a single line and adding an import statement.

Start by setting up your development environment. For all of the exercises, you will need to be able to compile and run Java code. I developed the examples using Java SE Development Kit 7. If you are using a more recent version, everything should still work. If you are using an older version, you might find some incompatibilities.

I recommend using an interactive development environment (IDE) that provides syntax checking, auto-completion, and source code refactoring. These features help you avoid errors or find them quickly. However, if you are preparing for a technical interview, remember that you will not have these tools during the interview, so you might also want to practice writing code without them.

If you have not already downloaded the code for this book, see the instructions in "Working with the Code" on page ix.

In the directory named code, you should find these files and directories:

- build.xml is an Ant file that makes it easier to compile and run the code.
- lib contains the libraries you'll need (for this exercise, just JUnit).
- src contains the source code.

If you navigate into src/com/allendowney/thinkdast, you'll find the source code for this exercise:

- ListClientExample.java contains the code from the previous section.
- ListClientExampleTest.java contains a JUnit test for ListClientExample.

Review ListClientExample and make sure you understand what it does. Then compile and run it. If you use Ant, you can navigate to the code directory and run ant ListClientExample.

You might get a warning like:

```
List is a raw type. References to generic type List<E>
should be parameterized.
```

To keep the example simple, I didn't bother to specify the type of the elements in the List. If this warning bothers you, you can fix it by replacing each List or LinkedList with List<Integer> or LinkedList<Integer>.

Review ListClientExampleTest. It runs one test, which creates a ListClientExample, invokes getList, and then checks whether the result is an ArrayList. Initially, this test will fail because the result is a LinkedList, not an ArrayList. Run this test and confirm that it fails.

NOTE: This test makes sense for this exercise, but it is not a good example of a test. Good tests should check whether the class under test satisfies the requirements of the *interface*; they should not depend on the details of the *implementation*.

In the ListClientExample, replace LinkedList with ArrayList. You might have to add an import statement. Compile and run ListClientExample. Then run the test again. With this change, the test should now pass.

To make this test pass, you only had to change `LinkedList` in the constructor; you did not have to change any of the places where `List` appears. What happens if you do? Go ahead and replace one or more appearances of `List` with `ArrayList`. The program should still work correctly, but now it is "overspecified". If you change your mind in the future and want to swap the interface again, you would have to change more code.

In the `ListClientExample` constructor, what happens if you replace `ArrayList` with `List`? Why can't you instantiate a `List`?

CHAPTER 2

Analysis of Algorithms

As we saw in the previous chapter, Java provides two implementations of the List interface, ArrayList and LinkedList. For some applications LinkedList is faster; for other applications ArrayList is faster.

To decide which one is better for a particular application, one approach is to try them both and see how long they take. This approach, which is called **profiling**, has a few problems:

1. Before you can compare the algorithms, you have to implement them both.

2. The results might depend on what kind of computer you use. One algorithm might be better on one machine; the other might be better on a different machine.

3. The results might depend on the size of the problem or the data provided as input.

We can address some of these problems using **analysis of algorithms**. When it works, algorithm analysis makes it possible to compare algorithms without having to implement them. But we have to make some assumptions:

1. To avoid dealing with the details of computer hardware, we usually identify the basic operations that make up an algorithm—like addition, multiplication, and comparison of numbers—and count the number of operations each algorithm requires.

2. To avoid dealing with the details of the input data, the best option is to analyze the average performance for the inputs we expect. If that's not possible, a common alternative is to analyze the worst case scenario.

3. Finally, we have to deal with the possibility that one algorithm works best for small problems and another for big ones. In that case, we usually focus on the big ones, because for small problems the difference probably doesn't matter, but for big problems the difference can be huge.

This kind of analysis lends itself to simple classification of algorithms. For example, if we know that the runtime of Algorithm A tends to be proportional to the size of the input, n, and Algorithm B tends to be proportional to n^2, we expect A to be faster than B, at least for large values of n.

Most simple algorithms fall into just a few categories:

Constant time

An algorithm is **constant time** if the runtime does not depend on the size of the input. For example, if you have an array of n elements and you use the bracket operator ([ ]) to access one of the elements, this operation takes the same number of operations regardless of how big the array is.

Linear

An algorithm is **linear** if the runtime is proportional to the size of the input. For example, if you add up the elements of an array, you have to access n elements and perform $n - 1$ additions. The total number of operations (element accesses and additions) is $2n - 1$, which is proportional to n.

Quadratic

An algorithm is **quadratic** if the runtime is proportional to n^2. For example, suppose you want to check whether any element in a list appears more than once. A simple algorithm is to compare each element to all of the others. If there are n elements and each is compared to $n - 1$ others, the total number of comparisons is $n^2 - n$, which is proportional to n^2 as n grows.

Selection Sort

For example, here's an implementation of a simple algorithm called **selection sort** (see *http://thinkdast.com/selectsort*):

```java
public class SelectionSort {

    /**
     * Swaps the elements at indexes i and j.
     */
    public static void swapElements(int[] array, int i, int j) {
        int temp = array[i];
        array[i] = array[j];
        array[j] = temp;
    }
```

```
/**
 * Finds the index of the lowest value
 * starting from the index at start (inclusive)
 * and going to the end of the array.
 */
public static int indexLowest(int[] array, int start) {
    int lowIndex = start;
    for (int i = start; i < array.length; i++) {
        if (array[i] < array[lowIndex]) {
            lowIndex = i;
        }
    }
    return lowIndex;
}

/**
 * Sorts the elements (in place) using selection sort.
 */
public static void selectionSort(int[] array) {
    for (int i = 0; i < array.length; i++) {
        int j = indexLowest(array, i);
        swapElements(array, i, j);
    }
}
}
```

The first method, swapElements, swaps two elements of the array. Reading and writing elements are constant time operations, because if we know the size of the elements and the location of the first, we can compute the location of any other element with one multiplication and one addition, and those are constant time operations. Since everything in swapElements is constant time, the whole method is constant time.

The second method, indexLowest, finds the index of the smallest element of the array starting at a given index, start. Each time through the loop, it accesses two elements of the array and performs one comparison. Since these are all constant time operations, it doesn't really matter which ones we count. To keep it simple, let's count the number of comparisons:

1. If start is 0, indexLowest traverses the entire array, and the total number of comparisons is the length of the array, which I'll call n.

2. If start is 1, the number of comparisons is $n - 1$.

3. In general, the number of comparisons is $n - start$, so indexLowest is linear.

The third method, selectionSort, sorts the array. It loops from 0 to $n - 1$, so the loop executes n times. Each time, it calls indexLowest and then performs a constant time operation, swapElements.

The first time `indexLowest` is called, it performs n comparisons. The second time, it performs $n - 1$ comparisons, and so on. The total number of comparisons is

$$n + n - 1 + n - 2 + \ldots + 1 + 0$$

The sum of this series is $n(n + 1)/2$, which is proportional to n^2; this means that `selectionSort` is quadratic.

To get to the same result a different way, we can think of `indexLowest` as a nested loop. Each time we call `indexLowest`, the number of operations is proportional to n. We call it n times, so the total number of operations is proportional to n^2.

Big O Notation

All constant time algorithms belong to a set called $O(1)$. So another way to say that an algorithm is constant time is to say that it is in $O(1)$. Similarly, all linear algorithms belong to $O(n)$, and all quadratic algorithms belong to $O(n^2)$. This way of classifying algorithms is called **big O notation**.

NOTE: I am providing a casual definition of big O notation. For a more mathematical treatment, see *http://thinkdast.com/bigo*.

This notation provides a convenient way to write general rules about how algorithms behave when we compose them. For example, if you perform a linear time algorithm followed by a constant algorithm, the total runtime is linear. Using $\in$ to mean "is a member of":

If $f \in O(n)$ and $g \in O(1)$, $f + g \in O(n)$.

If you perform two linear operations, the total is still linear:

If $f \in O(n)$ and $g \in O(n)$, $f + g \in O(n)$.

In fact, if you perform a linear operation any number of times, k, the total is linear, as long as k is a constant that does not depend on n:

If $f \in O(n)$ and k is a constant, $kf \in O(n)$.

But if you perform a linear operation n times, the result is quadratic:

If $f \in O(n)$, $nf \in O(n^2)$.

In general, we only care about the largest exponent of n. So if the total number of operations is $2n + 1$, it belongs to $O(n)$. The leading constant, 2, and the additive term, 1, are not important for this kind of analysis. Similarly, $n^2 + 100n + 1000$ is in $O(n^2)$. Don't be distracted by the big numbers!

Order of growth is another name for the same idea. An order of growth is a set of algorithms whose runtimes are in the same big O category; for example, all linear algorithms belong to the same order of growth because their runtimes are in $O(n)$.

In this context, an "order" is a group, like the *Order of the Knights of the Round Table*, which is a group of knights, not a way of lining them up. So you can imagine the *Order of Linear Algorithms* as a set of brave, chivalrous, and particularly efficient algorithms.

Exercise 2

The exercise for this chapter is to implement a List that uses a Java array to store the elements.

In the code repository for this book (see "Working with the Code" on page ix), you'll find the source files you'll need:

- MyArrayList.java contains a partial implementation of the List interface. Four of the methods are incomplete; your job is to fill them in.
- MyArrayListTest.java contains JUnit tests you can use to check your work.

You'll also find the Ant build file build.xml. From the code directory, you should be able to run ant MyArrayList to run MyArrayList.java, which contains a few simple tests. Or you can run ant MyArrayListTest to run the JUnit test.

When you run the tests, several of them should fail. If you examine the source code, you'll find four TODO comments indicating the methods you should fill in.

Before you start filling in the missing methods, let's walk through some of the code. Here are the class definition, instance variables, and constructor:

```
public class MyArrayList<E> implements List<E> {
    int size;                // keeps track of the number of elements
    private E[] array;       // stores the elements

    public MyArrayList() {
        array = (E[]) new Object[10];
        size = 0;
    }
}
```

As the comments indicate, size keeps track of how many elements are in MyArray List, and array is the array that actually contains the elements.

The constructor creates an array of 10 elements, which are initially null, and sets size to 0. Most of the time, the length of the array is bigger than size, so there are unused slots in the array.

One detail about Java: you can't instantiate an array using a type parameter; for example, the following will not work:

```
array = new E[10];
```

To work around this limitation, you have to instantiate an array of Object and then typecast it. You can read more about this issue at *http://thinkdast.com/generics*.

Next we'll look at the method that adds elements to the list:

```
public boolean add(E element) {
    if (size >= array.length) {
        // make a bigger array and copy over the elements
        E[] bigger = (E[]) new Object[array.length * 2];
        System.arraycopy(array, 0, bigger, 0, array.length);
        array = bigger;
    }
    array[size] = element;
    size++;
    return true;
}
```

If there are no unused spaces in the array, we have to create a bigger array and copy over the elements. Then we can store the element in the array and increment size.

It might not be obvious why this method returns a boolean, since it seems like it always returns true. As always, you can find the answer in the documentation: *http://thinkdast.com/colladd*. It's also not obvious how to analyze the performance of this method. In the normal case, it's constant time, but if we have to resize the array, it's linear. I'll explain how to handle this in "Classifying add" on page 17.

Finally, let's look at get; then you can get started on the exercise:

```
public T get(int index) {
    if (index < 0 || index >= size) {
        throw new IndexOutOfBoundsException();
    }
    return array[index];
}
```

Actually, get is pretty simple: if the index is out of bounds, it throws an exception; otherwise it reads and returns an element of the array. Notice that it checks whether the index is less than size, not array.length, so it's not possible to access the unused elements of the array.

In MyArrayList.java, you'll find a stub for set that looks like this:

```
public T set(int index, T element) {
    // TODO: fill in this method.
    return null;
}
```

Read the documentation of set at *http://thinkdast.com/listset*, then fill in the body of this method. If you run MyArrayListTest again, testSet should pass.

HINT: Try to avoid repeating the index-checking code.

Your next mission is to fill in indexOf. As usual, you should read the documentation at *http://thinkdast.com/listindof* so you know what it's supposed to do. In particular, notice how it is supposed to handle null.

I've provided a helper method called equals that compares an element from the array to a target value and returns true if they are equal (and it handles null correctly). Notice that this method is private because it is only used inside this class; it is not part of the List interface.

When you are done, run MyArrayListTest again; testIndexOf should pass now, as well as the other tests that depend on it.

Only two more methods to go, and you'll be done with this exercise. The next one is an overloaded version of add that takes an index and stores the new value at the given index, shifting the other elements to make room, if necessary.

Again, read the documentation at *http://thinkdast.com/listadd*, write an implementation, and run the tests for confirmation.

HINT: Avoid repeating the code that makes the array bigger.

Last one: fill in the body of remove. The documentation is at *http://thinkdast.com/listrem*. When you finish this one, all tests should pass.

Once you have your implementation working, compare it to mine, which you can read at *http://thinkdast.com/myarraylist*.

CHAPTER 3

ArrayList

This chapter kills two birds with one stone: I present solutions to the previous exercise and demonstrate a way to classify algorithms using **amortized analysis**.

Classifying MyArrayList Methods

For many methods, we can identify the order of growth by examining the code. For example, here's the implementation of `get` from `MyArrayList`:

```java
public E get(int index) {
    if (index < 0 || index >= size) {
        throw new IndexOutOfBoundsException();
    }
    return array[index];
}
```

Everything in `get` is constant time, so `get` is constant time. No problem.

Now that we've classified `get`, we can classify `set`, which uses it. Here is our implementation of `set` from the previous exercise:

```java
public E set(int index, E element) {
    E old = get(index);
    array[index] = element;
    return old;
}
```

One slightly clever part of this solution is that it does not check the bounds of the array explicitly; it takes advantage of `get`, which raises an exception if the index is invalid.

Everything in `set`, including the invocation of `get`, is constant time, so `set` is also constant time.

Next we'll look at some linear methods. For example, here's my implementation of `indexOf`:

```
public int indexOf(Object target) {
    for (int i = 0; i<size; i++) {
        if (equals(target, array[i])) {
            return i;
        }
    }
    return -1;
}
```

Each time through the loop, `indexOf` invokes `equals`, so we have to classify `equals` first. Here it is:

```
private boolean equals(Object target, Object element) {
    if (target == null) {
        return element == null;
    } else {
        return target.equals(element);
    }
}
```

This method invokes `target.equals`; the runtime of this method might depend on the size of `target` or `element`, but it probably doesn't depend on the size of the array, so we consider it constant time for purposes of analyzing `indexOf`.

Getting back to `indexOf`, everything inside the loop is constant time, so the next question we have to consider is: how many times does the loop execute?

If we get lucky, we might find the target object right away and return after testing only one element. If we are unlucky, we might have to test all of the elements. On average, we expect to test half of the elements, so this method is considered linear (except in the unlikely case that we know the target element is at the beginning of the array).

The analysis of `remove` is similar. Here's my implementation:

```
public E remove(int index) {
    E element = get(index);
    for (int i=index; i<size-1; i++) {
        array[i] = array[i+1];
    }
    size--;
    return element;
}
```

It uses `get`, which is constant time, and then loops through the array, starting from `index`. If we remove the element at the end of the list, the loop never runs and this method is constant time. If we remove the first element, we loop through all of the remaining elements, which is linear. So, again, this method is considered linear (except in the special case where we know the element is at the end or a constant distance from the end).

Classifying add

Here's a version of add that takes an index and an element as parameters:

```java
public void add(int index, E element) {
    if (index < 0 || index > size) {
        throw new IndexOutOfBoundsException();
    }
    // add the element to get the resizing
    add(element);

    // shift the other elements
    for (int i=size-1; i>index; i--) {
        array[i] = array[i-1];
    }
    // put the new one in the right place
    array[index] = element;
}
```

This two-parameter version, called add(int, E), uses the one-parameter version, called add(E), which puts the new element at the end. Then it shifts the other elements to the right, and puts the new element in the correct place.

Before we can classify the two-parameter add(int, E), we have to classify the one-parameter add(E):

```java
public boolean add(E element) {
    if (size >= array.length) {
        // make a bigger array and copy over the elements
        E[] bigger = (E[]) new Object[array.length * 2];
        System.arraycopy(array, 0, bigger, 0, array.length);
        array = bigger;
    }
    array[size] = element;
    size++;
    return true;
}
```

The one-parameter version turns out to be hard to analyze. If there is an unused space in the array, it is constant time, but if we have to resize the array, it's linear because System.arraycopy takes time proportional to the size of the array.

So is add constant time or linear? We can classify this method by thinking about the average number of operations per add over a series of n adds. For simplicity, assume we start with an array that has room for 2 elements:

- The first time we call add, it finds unused space in the array, so it stores 1 element.

- The second time, it finds unused space in the array, so it stores 1 element.

- The third time, we have to resize the array, copy 2 elements, and store 1 element. Now the size of the array is 4.

- The fourth time stores 1 element.

- The fifth time resizes the array, copies 4 elements, and stores 1 element. Now the size of the array is 8.

- The next 3 adds store 3 elements.

- The next add copies 8 and stores 1. Now the size is 16.

- The next 7 adds store 7 elements.

And so on. Adding things up:

- After 4 adds, we've stored 4 elements and copied 2.

- After 8 adds, we've stored 8 elements and copied 6.

- After 16 adds, we've stored 16 elements and copied 14.

By now you should see the pattern: to do n adds, we have to store n elements and copy $n - 2$. So the total number of operations is $n + n - 2$, which is $2n - 2$.

To get the average number of operations per add, we divide the total by n; the result is $2 - 2/n$. As n gets big, the second term, $2/n$, gets small. Invoking the principle that we only care about the largest exponent of n, we can think of add as constant time.

It might seem strange that an algorithm that is sometimes linear can be constant time on average. The key is that we double the length of the array each time it gets resized. That limits the number of times each element gets copied. Otherwise—if we add a fixed amount to the length of the array, rather than multiplying by a fixed amount—the analysis doesn't work.

This way of classifying an algorithm, by computing the average time in a series of invocations, is called **amortized analysis**. You can read more about it at *http://think dast.com/amort*. The key idea is that the extra cost of copying the array is spread, or "amortized", over a series of invocations.

Now, if add(E) is constant time, what about add(int, E)? After calling add(E), it loops through part of the array and shifts elements. This loop is linear, except in the special case where we are adding at the end of the list. So add(int, E) is linear.

Problem Size

The last example we'll consider is removeAll; here's the implementation in MyArray
List:

```java
public boolean removeAll(Collection<?> collection) {
    boolean flag = true;
    for (Object obj: collection) {
        flag &= remove(obj);
    }
    return flag;
}
```

Each time through the loop, removeAll invokes remove, which is linear. So it is
tempting to think that removeAll is quadratic. But that's not necessarily the case.

In this method, the loop runs once for each element in collection. If collection
contains m elements and the list we are removing from contains n elements, this
method is in $O(nm)$. If the size of collection can be considered constant, removeAll
is linear with respect to n. But if the size of the collection is proportional to n, remove
All is quadratic. For example, if collection always contains 100 or fewer elements,
removeAll is linear. But if collection generally contains 1% of the elements in the
list, removeAll is quadratic.

When we talk about **problem size**, we have to be careful about which size, or sizes, we
are talking about. This example demonstrates a pitfall of algorithm analysis: the
tempting shortcut of counting loops. If there is one loop, the algorithm is *often* linear.
If there are two loops (one nested inside the other), the algorithm is *often* quadratic.
But be careful! You have to think about how many times each loop runs. If the number of iterations is proportional to n for all loops, you can get away with just counting
the loops. But if, as in this example, the number of iterations is not always proportional to n, you have to give it more thought.

Linked Data Structures

For the next exercise I provide a partial implementation of the List interface that
uses a linked list to store the elements. If you are not familiar with linked lists, you
can read about them at *http://thinkdast.com/linkedlist*, but this section provides a brief
introduction.

A data structure is "linked" if it is made up of objects, often called "nodes", that contain references to other nodes. In a linked *list*, each node contains a reference to the
next node in the list. Other linked structures include trees and graphs, in which nodes
can contain references to more than one other node.

Here's a class definition for a simple node:

```java
public class ListNode {

    public Object data;
    public ListNode next;

    public ListNode() {
        this.data = null;
        this.next = null;
    }

    public ListNode(Object data) {
        this.data = data;
        this.next = null;
    }

    public ListNode(Object data, ListNode next) {
        this.data = data;
        this.next = next;
    }

    public String toString() {
        return "ListNode(" + data.toString() + ")";
    }
}
```

The ListNode object has two instance variables: data is a reference to some kind of Object, and next is a reference to the next node in the list. In the last node in the list, by convention, next is null.

ListNode provides several constructors, allowing you to provide values for data and next, or initialize them to the default value, null.

You can think of each ListNode as a list with a single element, but more generally, a list can contain any number of nodes. There are several ways to make a new list. A simple option is to create a set of ListNode objects, like this:

```java
ListNode node1 = new ListNode(1);
ListNode node2 = new ListNode(2);
ListNode node3 = new ListNode(3);
```

And then link them up, like this:

```java
node1.next = node2;
node2.next = node3;
node3.next = null;
```

Alternatively, you can create a node and link it at the same time. For example, if you want to add a new node at the beginning of a list, you can do it like this:

```java
ListNode node0 = new ListNode(0, node1);
```

After this sequence of instructions, we have four nodes containing the Integers 0, 1, 2, and 3 as data, linked up in increasing order. In the last node, the next field is null.

Figure 3-1 is an object diagram that shows these variables and the objects they refer to. In an object diagram, variables appear as names inside boxes, with arrows that show what they refer to. Objects appear as boxes with their type on the outside (like ListNode and Integer) and their instance variables on the inside.

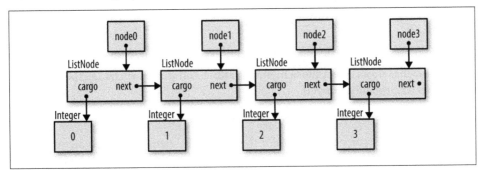

Figure 3-1. Object diagram of a linked list.

Exercise 3

In the repository for this book, you'll find the source files you need for this exercise:

- MyLinkedList.java contains a partial implementation of the List interface using a linked list to store the elements.
- MyLinkedListTest.java contains JUnit tests for MyLinkedList.

Run ant MyArrayList to run MyArrayList.java, which contains a few simple tests.

Then you can run ant MyArrayListTest to run the JUnit tests. Several of them should fail. If you examine the source code, you'll find three TODO comments indicating the methods you should fill in.

Before you start, let's walk through some of the code. Here are the instance variables and the constructor for MyLinkedList:

```
public class MyLinkedList<E> implements List<E> {

    private int size;          // keeps track of the number of elements
    private Node head;         // reference to the first node

    public MyLinkedList() {
        head = null;
        size = 0;
    }
}
```

As the comments indicate, size keeps track of how many elements are in MyLinked List; head is a reference to the first Node in the list or null if the list is empty.

Storing the number of elements is not necessary, and in general it is risky to keep redundant information, because if it's not updated correctly, it creates opportunities for error. It also takes a little bit of extra space.

But if we store size explicitly, we can implement the size method in constant time; otherwise, we would have to traverse the list and count the elements, which requires linear time.

Because we store size explicitly, we have to update it each time we add or remove an element, so that slows down those methods a little, but it doesn't change their order of growth, so it's probably worth it.

The constructor sets head to null, which indicates an empty list, and sets size to 0.

This class uses the type parameter E for the type of the elements. If you are not familiar with type parameters, you might want to read this tutorial: *http://thinkdast.com/types*.

The type parameter also appears in the definition of Node, which is nested inside MyLinkedList:

```
private class Node {
    public E data;
    public Node next;

    public Node(E data, Node next) {
        this.data = data;
        this.next = next;
    }
}
```

Other than that, Node is similar to ListNode in "Linked Data Structures" on page 19.

Finally, here's my implementation of add:

```
public boolean add(E element) {
    if (head == null) {
        head = new Node(element);
    } else {
        Node node = head;
        // loop until the last node
        for ( ; node.next != null; node = node.next) {}
        node.next = new Node(element);
    }
    size++;
    return true;
}
```

This example demonstrates two patterns you'll need for your solutions:

1. For many methods, we have to handle the first element of the list as a special case. In this example, if we are adding the first element of a list, we have to modify head. Otherwise, we traverse the list, find the end, and add the new node.

2. This method shows how to use a for loop to traverse the nodes in a list. In your solutions, you will probably write several variations on this loop. Notice that we have to declare node before the loop so we can access it after the loop.

Now it's your turn. Fill in the body of indexOf. As usual, you should read the documentation, at *http://thinkdast.com/listindof*, so you know what it is supposed to do. In particular, notice how it's supposed to handle null.

As in the previous exercise, I provide a helper method called equals that compares an element from the array to a target value and checks whether they are equal—and it handles null correctly. This method is private because it is used inside this class but it is not part of the List interface.

When you are done, run the tests again; testIndexOf should pass now, as well as the other tests that depend on it.

Next, you should fill in the two-parameter version of add, which takes an index and stores the new value at the given index. Again, read the documentation at *http://think dast.com/listadd*, write an implementation, and run the tests for confirmation.

Last one: fill in the body of remove. The documentation is here: *http://thinkdast.com/listrem*. When you finish this one, all tests should pass.

Once you have your implementation working, compare it to the version in the solution directory of the repository.

A Note on Garbage Collection

In MyArrayList from the previous exercise, the array grows if necessary, but it never shrinks. The array never gets garbage collected, and the elements don't get garbage collected until the list itself is destroyed.

One advantage of the linked list implementation is that it shrinks when elements are removed, and the unused nodes can get garbage collected immediately.

Here is my implementation of the clear method:

```
public void clear() {
    head = null;
    size = 0;
}
```

When we set head to null, we remove a reference to the first Node. If there are no other references to that Node (and there shouldn't be), it will get garbage collected. At that point, the reference to the second Node is removed, so it gets garbage collected, too. This process continues until all nodes are collected.

So how should we classify clear? The method itself contains two constant time operations, so it sure looks like it's constant time. But when you invoke it, you make the garbage collector do work that's proportional to the number of elements. So maybe we should consider it linear!

This is an example of what is sometimes called a **performance bug**: a program that is correct in the sense that it does the right thing, but it doesn't belong to the order of growth we expected. In languages like Java that do a lot of work, like garbage collection, behind the scenes, this kind of bug can be hard to find.

CHAPTER 4

LinkedList

This chapter presents solutions to the previous exercise and continues the discussion of analysis of algorithms.

Classifying MyLinkedList Methods

My implementation of indexOf is the following code snippet. Read through it and see if you can identify its order of growth before you read the explanation:

```java
public int indexOf(Object target) {
    Node node = head;
    for (int i=0; i<size; i++) {
        if (equals(target, node.data)) {
            return i;
        }
        node = node.next;
    }
    return -1;
}
```

Initially node gets a copy of head, so they both refer to the same Node. The loop variable, i, counts from 0 to size-1. Each time through the loop, we use equals to see if we've found the target. If so, we return i immediately. Otherwise we advance to the next Node in the list.

Normally we would check to make sure the next Node is not null, but in this case it is safe because the loop ends when we get to the end of the list (assuming size is consistent with the actual number of nodes in the list).

If we get through the loop without finding the target, we return -1.

So what is the order of growth for this method?

1. Each time through the loop we invoke `equals`, which is constant time (it might depend on the size of `target` or `data`, but it doesn't depend on the size of the list). The other operations in the loop are also constant time.

2. The loop might run *n* times, because in the worse case, we might have to traverse the whole list.

So the runtime of this method is proportional to the length of the list.

Next, here is my implementation of the two-parameter `add` method. Again, you should try to classify it before you read the explanation:

```java
public void add(int index, E element) {
    if (index == 0) {
        head = new Node(element, head);
    } else {
        Node node = getNode(index-1);
        node.next = new Node(element, node.next);
    }
    size++;
}
```

If `index==0`, we're adding the new `Node` at the beginning, so we handle that as a special case. Otherwise, we have to traverse the list to find the element at `index-1`. We use the helper method `getNode`:

```java
private Node getNode(int index) {
    if (index < 0 || index >= size) {
        throw new IndexOutOfBoundsException();
    }
    Node node = head;
    for (int i=0; i<index; i++) {
        node = node.next;
    }
    return node;
}
```

`getNode` checks whether `index` is out of bounds; if so, it throws an exception. Otherwise it traverses the list and returns the requested `Node`.

Jumping back to `add`, once we find the right `Node`, we create the new `Node` and put it between `node` and `node.next`. You might find it helpful to draw a diagram of this operation to make sure you understand it.

So, what's the order of growth for `add`?

1. `getNode` is similar to `indexOf`, and it is linear for the same reason.

2. In `add`, everything before and after `getNode` is constant time.

So all together, `add` is linear.

Finally, let's look at remove:

```
public E remove(int index) {
    E element = get(index);
    if (index == 0) {
        head = head.next;
    } else {
        Node node = getNode(index-1);
        node.next = node.next.next;
    }
    size--;
    return element;
}
```

remove uses get to find and store the element at index. Then it removes the Node that contained it.

If index==0, we handle that as a special case again. Otherwise we find the node at index-1 and modify it to skip over node.next and link directly to node.next.next. This effectively removes node.next from the list, and it can be garbage collected.

Finally, we decrement size and return the element we retrieved at the beginning.

So, what's the order of growth for remove? Everything in remove is constant time except get and getNode, which are linear. So remove is linear.

When people see two linear operations, they sometimes think the result is quadratic, but that only applies if one operation is nested inside the other. If you invoke one operation after the other, the runtimes add. If they are both in $O(n)$, the sum is also in $O(n)$.

Comparing MyArrayList and MyLinkedList

The following table summarizes the differences between MyLinkedList and MyArray List, where 1 means $O(1)$ or constant time and n means $O(n)$ or linear:

	MyArrayList	MyLinkedList
add (at the end)	1	n
add (at the beginning)	n	1
add (in general)	n	n
get / set	1	n
indexOf / lastIndexOf	n	n
isEmpty / size	1	1
remove (from the end)	1	n
remove (from the beginning)	n	1
remove (in general)	n	n

The operations where `MyArrayList` has an advantage are adding at the end, removing from the end, getting and setting.

The operations where `MyLinkedList` has an advantage are adding at the beginning and removing from the beginning.

For the other operations, the two implementations are in the same order of growth.

Which implementation is better? It depends on which operations you are likely to use the most. And that's why Java provides more than one implementation, because it depends.

Profiling

For the next exercise I provide a class called `Profiler` that contains code that runs a method with a range of problem sizes, measures runtimes, and plots the results.

You will use `Profiler` to classify the performance of the `add` method for the Java implementations of `ArrayList` and `LinkedList`.

Here's an example that shows how to use the profiler:

```
public static void profileArrayListAddEnd() {
    Timeable timeable = new Timeable() {
        List<String> list;

        public void setup(int n) {
            list = new ArrayList<String>();
        }

        public void timeMe(int n) {
            for (int i=0; i<n; i++) {
                list.add("a string");
            }
        }
    };

    String title = "ArrayList add end";
    Profiler profiler = new Profiler(title, timeable);

    int startN = 4000;
    int endMillis = 1000;
    XYSeries series = profiler.timingLoop(startN, endMillis);
    profiler.plotResults(series);
}
```

This method measures the time it takes to run `add` on an `ArrayList`, which adds the new element at the end. I'll explain the code and then show the results.

In order to use `Profiler`, we need to create a `Timeable` object that provides two methods: `setup` and `timeMe`. The `setup` method does whatever needs to be done before we start the clock; in this case it creates an empty list. Then `timeMe` does whatever operation we are trying to measure; in this case it adds *n* elements to the list.

The code that creates `timeable` is an **anonymous class** that defines a new implementation of the `Timeable` interface and creates an instance of the new class at the same time. If you are not familiar with anonymous classes, you can read about them here: *http://thinkdast.com/anonclass*.

But you don't need to know much for the next exercise; even if you are not comfortable with anonymous classes, you can copy and modify the example code.

The next step is to create the `Profiler` object, passing the `Timeable` object and a title as parameters.

The `Profiler` provides `timingLoop` which uses the `Timeable` object stored as an instance variable. It invokes the `timeMe` method on the `Timeable` object several times with a range of values of *n*. `timingLoop` takes two parameters:

- `startN` is the value of *n* the timing loop should start at.
- `endMillis` is a threshold in milliseconds. As `timingLoop` increases the problem size, the runtime increases; when the runtime exceeds this threshold, `timingLoop` stops.

When you run the experiments, you might have to adjust these parameters. If `startN` is too low, the runtime might be too short to measure accurately. If `endMillis` is too low, you might not get enough data to see a clear relationship between problem size and runtime.

This code is in `ProfileListAdd.java`, which you'll run in the next exercise. When I ran it, I got this output:

```
4000, 3
8000, 0
16000, 1
32000, 2
64000, 3
128000, 6
256000, 18
512000, 30
1024000, 88
2048000, 185
4096000, 242
8192000, 544
16384000, 1325
```

The first column is problem size, *n*; the second column is runtime in milliseconds. The first few measurements are pretty noisy; it might have been better to set startN around 64000.

The result from timingLoop is an XYSeries that contains this data. If you pass this series to plotResults, it generates a plot like the one in Figure 4-1.

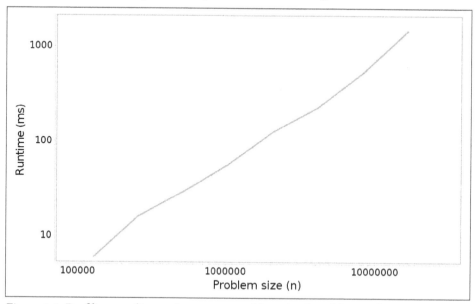

Figure 4-1. Profiling results: runtime versus problem size for adding n elements to the end of an ArrayList.

The next section explains how to interpret it.

Interpreting Results

Based on our understanding of how ArrayList works, we expect the add method to take constant time when we add elements to the end. So the total time to add *n* elements should be linear.

To test that theory, we could plot total runtime versus problem size, and we should see a straight line, at least for problem sizes that are big enough to measure accurately. Mathematically, we can write the function for that line:

runtime = *a* + *bn*

where *a* is the intercept of the line and *b* is the slope.

On the other hand, if add is linear, the total time for n adds would be quadratic. If we plot runtime versus problem size, we expect to see a parabola. Or mathematically, something like:

$$\text{runtime} = a + bn + cn^2$$

With perfect data, we might be able to tell the difference between a straight line and a parabola, but if the measurements are noisy, it can be hard to tell. A better way to interpret noisy measurements is to plot runtime and problem size on a **log-log** scale.

Why? Let's suppose that runtime is proportional to n^k, but we don't know what the exponent k is. We can write the relationship like this:

$$\text{runtime} = a + bn + \ldots + cn^k$$

For large values of n, the term with the largest exponent is the most important, so:

$$\text{runtime} \approx cn^k$$

where $\approx$ means "approximately equal". Now, if we take the logarithm of both sides of this equation:

$$\log(\text{runtime}) \approx \log(c) + k \log(n)$$

This equation implies that if we plot runtime versus n on a log-log scale, we expect to see a straight line with intercept $\log(c)$ and slope k. We don't care much about the intercept, but the slope indicates the order of growth: if $k = 1$, the algorithm is linear; if $k = 2$, it's quadratic.

Looking at the figure in the previous section, you can estimate the slope by eye. But when you call plotResults it computes a least squares fit to the data and prints the estimated slope. In this example:

```
Estimated slope = 1.06194352346708
```

which is close to 1; and that suggests that the total time for n adds is linear, so each add is constant time, as expected.

One important point: if you see a straight line on a graph like this, that does *not* mean that the algorithm is linear. If the runtime is proportional to n^k for any exponent k, we expect to see a straight line with slope k. If the slope is close to 1, that suggests the algorithm is linear. If it is close to 2, it's probably quadratic.

Exercise 4

In the repository for this book you'll find the source files you need for this exercise:

1. `Profiler.java` contains the implementation of the `Profiler` class described in the previous section. You will use this class, but you don't have to know how it works. But feel free to read the source.

2. `ProfileListAdd.java` contains starter code for this exercise, including the example in the previous section. You will modify this file to profile a few other methods.

Also, in the code directory, you'll find the Ant build file `build.xml`.

1. Run `ant ProfileListAdd` to run `ProfileListAdd.java`. You should get results similar to Figure 4-1, but you might have to adjust `startN` or `endMillis`. The estimated slope should be close to 1, indicating that performing n add operations takes time proportional to n raised to the exponent 1; that is, it is in $O(n)$.

2. In `ProfileListAdd.java`, you'll find an empty method named `profileArrayLis tAddBeginning`. Fill in the body of this method with code that tests `Array List.add`, always putting the new element at the beginning. If you start with a copy of `profileArrayListAddEnd`, you should only have to make a few changes. Add a line in `main` to invoke this method.

3. Run `ant ProfileListAdd` again and interpret the results. Based on our understanding of how `ArrayList` works, we expect each add operation to be linear, so the total time for n adds should be quadratic. If so, the estimated slope of the line, on a log-log scale, should be near 2. Is it?

4. Now let's compare that to the performance of `LinkedList`. Fill in the body of `pro fileLinkedListAddBeginning` and use it to classify `LinkedList.add` when we put the new element at the beginning. What performance do you expect? Are the results consistent with your expectations?

5. Finally, fill in the body of `profileLinkedListAddEnd` and use it to classify `Linked List.add` when we put the new element at the end. What performance do you expect? Are the results consistent with your expectations?

I'll present results and answer these questions in the next chapter.

CHAPTER 5

Doubly Linked List

This chapter reviews results from the previous exercise and introduces yet another implementation of the List interface, the doubly linked list.

Performance Profiling Results

In the previous exercise, we used Profiler.java to run various ArrayList and Link edList operations with a range of problem sizes. We plotted runtime versus problem size on a log-log scale and estimated the slope of the resulting curve, which indicates the leading exponent of the relationship between runtime and problem size.

For example, when we used the add method to add elements to the end of an Array List, we found that the total time to perform n adds was proportional to n; that is, the estimated slope was close to 1. We concluded that performing n adds is in $O(n)$, so on average the time for a single add is constant time, or $O(1)$, which is what we expect based on algorithm analysis.

The exercise asks you to fill in the body of profileArrayListAddBeginning, which tests the performance of adding new elements at the beginning of an ArrayList. Based on our analysis, we expect each add to be linear, because it has to shift the other elements to the right; so we expect n adds to be quadratic.

Here's a solution, which you can find in the solution directory of the repository:

```java
public static void profileArrayListAddBeginning() {
    Timeable timeable = new Timeable() {
        List<String> list;

        public void setup(int n) {
            list = new ArrayList<String>();
        }
```

```
            public void timeMe(int n) {
                for (int i=0; i<n; i++) {
                    list.add(0, "a string");
                }
            }
        };
        int startN = 4000;
        int endMillis = 10000;
        runProfiler("ArrayList add beginning", timeable, startN, endMillis);
    }
```

This method is almost identical to profileArrayListAddEnd. The only difference is in timeMe, which uses the two-parameter version of add to put the new element at index 0. Also, we increased endMillis to get one additional data point.

Here are the timing results (problem size on the left, runtime in milliseconds on the right):

```
4000, 14
8000, 35
16000, 150
32000, 604
64000, 2518
128000, 11555
```

Figure 5-1 shows the graph of runtime versus problem size.

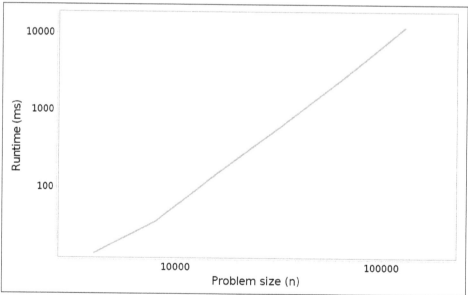

Figure 5-1. Profiling results: runtime versus problem size for adding n elements at the beginning of an ArrayList.

Remember that a straight line on this graph does *not* mean that the algorithm is linear. Rather, if the runtime is proportional to n^k for any exponent, k, we expect to see a straight line with slope k. In this case, we expect the total time for n adds to be proportional to n^2, so we expect a straight line with slope 2. In fact, the estimated slope is 1.992, which is so close I would be afraid to fake data this good.

Profiling LinkedList Methods

In the previous exercise you also profiled the performance of adding new elements at the beginning of a LinkedList. Based on our analysis, we expect each add to take constant time, because in a linked list, we don't have to shift the existing elements; we can just add a new node at the beginning. So we expect the total time for n adds to be linear.

Here's a solution:

```
public static void profileLinkedListAddBeginning() {
    Timeable timeable = new Timeable() {
        List<String> list;

        public void setup(int n) {
            list = new LinkedList<String>();
        }

        public void timeMe(int n) {
            for (int i=0; i<n; i++) {
                list.add(0, "a string");
            }
        }
    };
    int startN = 128000;
    int endMillis = 2000;
    runProfiler("LinkedList add beginning", timeable, startN, endMillis);
}
```

We only had a make a few changes, replacing ArrayList with LinkedList and adjusting startN and endMillis to get a good range of data. The measurements were noisier than the previous batch; here are the results:

```
128000, 16
256000, 19
512000, 28
1024000, 77
2048000, 330
4096000, 892
8192000, 1047
16384000, 4755
```

Figure 5-2 shows the graph of these results.

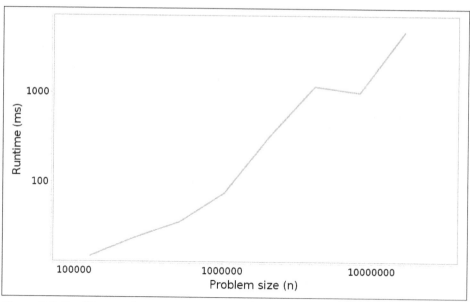

Figure 5-2. Profiling results: runtime versus problem size for adding n elements at the beginning of a LinkedList.

It's not a very straight line, and the slope is not exactly 1; the slope of the least squares fit is 1.23. But these results indicate that the total time for *n* adds is at least approximately $O(n)$, so each add is constant time.

Adding to the End of a LinkedList

Adding elements at the beginning is one of the operations where we expect Linked List to be faster than ArrayList. But for adding elements at the end, we expect LinkedList to be slower. In my implementation, we have to traverse the entire list to add an element to the end, which is linear. So we expect the total time for *n* adds to be quadratic.

Well, it's not. Here's the code:

```
public static void profileLinkedListAddEnd() {
    Timeable timeable = new Timeable() {
        List<String> list;

        public void setup(int n) {
            list = new LinkedList<String>();
        }

        public void timeMe(int n) {
            for (int i=0; i<n; i++) {
                list.add("a string");
            }
        }
    };
    int startN = 64000;
    int endMillis = 1000;
    runProfiler("LinkedList add end", timeable, startN, endMillis);
}
```

Here are the results:

```
64000, 9
128000, 9
256000, 21
512000, 24
1024000, 78
2048000, 235
4096000, 851
8192000, 950
16384000, 6160
```

Figure 5-3 shows the graph of these results.

Again, the measurements are noisy and the line is not perfectly straight, but the estimated slope is 1.19, which is close to what we got adding elements at the beginning, and not very close to 2, which is what we expected based on our analysis. In fact, it is closer to 1, which suggests that adding elements at the end is constant time. What's going on?

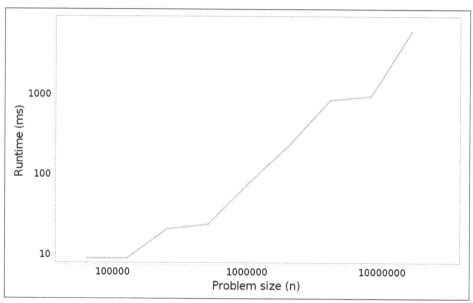

Figure 5-3. Profiling results: runtime versus problem size for adding n elements at the end of a LinkedList.

Doubly Linked List

My implementation of a linked list, MyLinkedList, uses a singly linked list; that is, each element contains a link to the next, and the MyArrayList object itself has a link to the first node.

But if you read the documentation of LinkedList at *http://thinkdast.com/linked*, it says:

> Doubly linked list implementation of the List and Deque interfaces....All of the operations perform as could be expected for a doubly linked list. Operations that index into the list will traverse the list from the beginning or the end, whichever is closer to the specified index.

If you are not familiar with doubly linked lists, you can read more about them at *http://thinkdast.com/doublelist*, but the short version is:

- Each node contains a link to the next node and a link to the previous node.
- The LinkedList object contains links to the first and last elements of the list.

So we can start at either end of the list and traverse it in either direction. As a result, we can add and remove elements from the beginning and the end of the list in constant time!

The following table summarizes the performance we expect from `ArrayList`, `MyLin kedList` (singly linked), and `LinkedList` (doubly linked):

	MyArrayList	MyLinkedList	LinkedList
add (at the end)	1	n	1
add (at the beginning)	n	1	1
add (in general)	n	n	n
get / set	1	n	n
indexOf / lastIndexOf	n	n	n
isEmpty / size	1	1	1
remove (from the end)	1	n	1
remove (from the beginning)	n	1	1
remove (in general)	n	n	n

Choosing a Structure

The doubly linked implementation is better than `ArrayList` for adding and removing at the beginning, and just as good as `ArrayList` for adding and removing at the end. So the only advantage of `ArrayList` is for get and set, which require linear time in a linked list, even if it is doubly linked.

If you know that the runtime of your application depends on the time it takes to get and set elements, an `ArrayList` might be the better choice. If the runtime depends on adding and removing elements near the beginning or the end, `LinkedList` might be better.

But remember that these recommendations are based on the order of growth for large problems. There are other factors to consider:

- If these operations don't take up a substantial fraction of the runtime for your application—that is, if your applications spends most of its time doing other things—then your choice of a `List` implementation won't matter very much.

- If the lists you are working with are not very big, you might not get the performance you expect. For small problems, a quadratic algorithm might be faster than a linear algorithm, or linear might be faster than constant time. And for small problems, the difference probably doesn't matter.

- Also, don't forget about space. So far we have focused on runtime, but different implementations require different amounts of space. In an `ArrayList`, the elements are stored side by side in a single chunk of memory, so there is little wasted space, and computer hardware is often faster with contiguous chunks. In a linked list, each element requires a node with one or two links. The links take up space (sometimes more than the data!), and with nodes scattered around in memory, the hardware might be less efficient.

In summary, analysis of algorithms provides some guidance for choosing data structures, but only if

1. The runtime of your application is important,

2. The runtime of your application depends on your choice of data structure, and

3. The problem size is large enough that the order of growth actually predicts which data structure is better.

You could have a long career as a software engineer without ever finding yourself in this situation.

CHAPTER 6

Tree Traversal

This chapter introduces the application we will develop during the rest of the book, a web search engine. I describe the elements of a search engine and introduce the first application, a web crawler that downloads and parses pages from Wikipedia. This chapter also presents a recursive implementation of depth-first search and an iterative implementation that uses a Java `Deque` to implement a "last in, first out" stack.

Search Engines

A **web search engine**, like Google Search or Bing, takes a set of search terms and returns a list of web pages that are relevant to those terms (I'll discuss what "relevant" means later). You can read more at *http://thinkdast.com/searcheng*, but I'll explain what you need as we go along.

The essential components of a search engine are:

Crawling
> We'll need a program that can download a web page, parse it, and extract the text and any links to other pages.

Indexing
> We'll need a data structure that makes it possible to look up a search term and find the pages that contain it.

Retrieval
> And we'll need a way to collect results from the index and identify pages that are most relevant to the search terms.

We'll start with the crawler. The goal of a crawler is to discover and download a set of web pages. For search engines like Google and Bing, the goal is to find *all* web pages, but often crawlers are limited to a smaller domain. In our case, we will only read pages from Wikipedia.

As a first step, we'll build a crawler that reads a Wikipedia page, finds the first link, follows the link to another page, and repeats. We will use this crawler to test the "Getting to Philosophy" conjecture, which states:

> Clicking on the first lowercase link in the main text of a Wikipedia article, and then repeating the process for subsequent articles, usually eventually gets one to the Philosophy article.

This conjecture is stated at *http://thinkdast.com/getphil*, and you can read its history there.

Testing the conjecture will allow us to build the basic pieces of a crawler without having to crawl the entire web, or even all of Wikipedia. And I think the exercise is kind of fun!

In a few chapters, we'll work on the indexer, and then we'll get to the retriever.

Parsing HTML

When you download a web page, the contents are written in HyperText Markup Language, aka HTML. For example, here is a minimal HTML document:

```
<!DOCTYPE html>
<html>
  <head>
    <title>This is a title</title>
  </head>
  <body>
    <p>Hello world!</p>
  </body>
</html>
```

The phrases "This is a title" and "Hello world!" are the text that actually appears on the page; the other elements are **tags** that indicate how the text should be displayed.

When our crawler downloads a page, it will need to parse the HTML in order to extract the text and find the links. To do that, we'll use **jsoup**, which is an open source Java library that downloads and parses HTML.

The result of parsing HTML is a Document Object Model tree, or **DOM tree**, that contains the elements of the document, including text and tags. The tree is a linked data structure made up of nodes; the nodes represent text, tags, and other document elements.

The relationships between the nodes are determined by the structure of the document. In the preceding example, the first node, called the **root**, is the <html> tag, which contains links to the two nodes it contains, <head> and <body>; these nodes are the **children** of the root node.

The <head> node has one child, <title>, and the <body> node has one child, <p> (which stands for "paragraph"). Figure 6-1 represents this tree graphically.

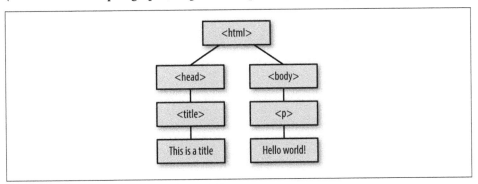

Figure 6-1. DOM tree for a simple HTML page.

Each node contains links to its children; in addition, each node contains a link to its **parent**, so from any node it is possible to navigate up and down the tree. The DOM tree for real pages is usually more complicated than this example.

Most web browsers provide tools for inspecting the DOM of the page you are viewing. In Chrome, you can right-click any part of a web page and select "Inspect" from the menu that pops up. In Firefox, you can right-click and select "Inspect Element" from the menu. Safari provides a tool called Web Inspector, which you can read about at *http://thinkdast.com/safari*. For Internet Explorer, you can read the instructions at *http://thinkdast.com/explorer*.

Figure 6-2 shows a screenshot of the DOM for the Wikipedia page on Java, *http://thinkdast.com/java*. The element that's highlighted is the first paragraph of the main text of the article, which is contained in a <div> element with id="mw-content-text". We'll use this element ID to identify the main text of each article we download.

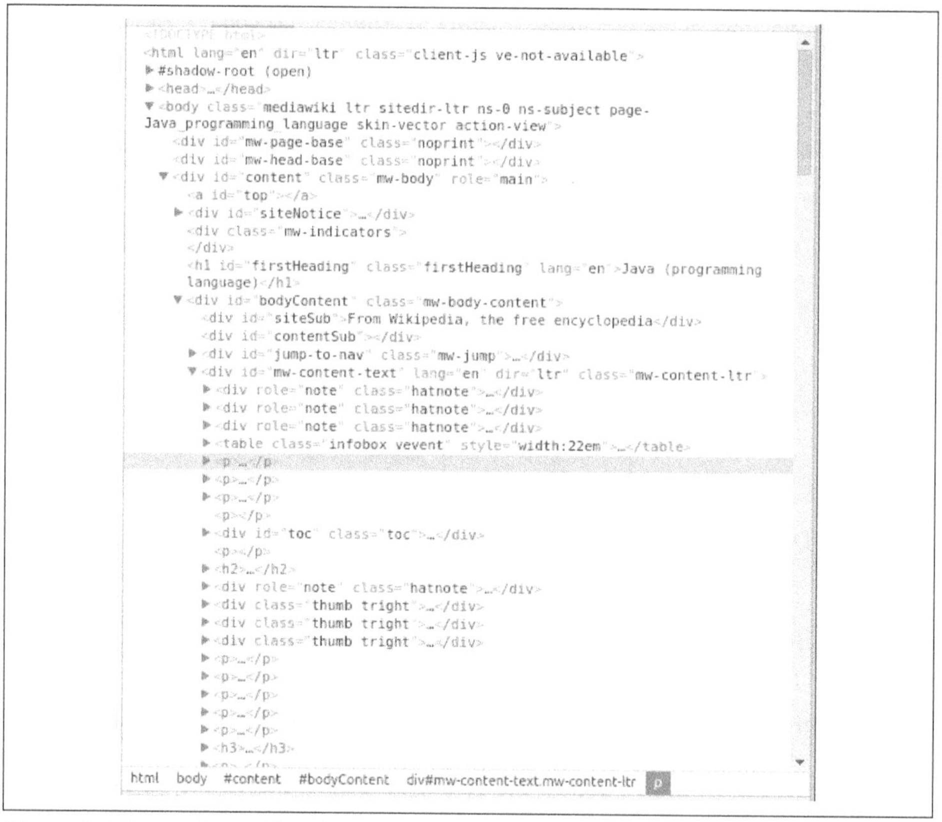

Figure 6-2. Screenshot of the Chrome DOM Inspector.

Using jsoup

jsoup makes it easy to download and parse web pages, and to navigate the DOM tree. Here's an example:

```
String url = "http://en.wikipedia.org/wiki/Java_(programming_language)";

// download and parse the document
Connection conn = Jsoup.connect(url);
Document doc = conn.get();

// select the content text and pull out the paragraphs.
Element content = doc.getElementById("mw-content-text");
Elements paragraphs = content.select("p");
```

Jsoup.connect takes a URL as a `String` and makes a connection to the web server; the `get` method downloads the HTML, parses it, and returns a `Document` object, which represents the DOM.

Document provides methods for navigating the tree and selecting nodes. In fact, it provides so many methods, it can be confusing. This example demonstrates two ways to select nodes:

- getElementById takes a String and searches the tree for an element that has a matching "id" field. Here it selects the node <div id="mw-content-text" lang="en" dir="ltr" class="mw-content-ltr">, which appears on every Wikipedia page to identify the <div> element that contains the main text of the page, as opposed to the navigation sidebar and other elements.

  The return value from getElementById is an Element object that represents this <div> and contains the elements in the <div> as children, grandchildren, etc.

- select takes a String, traverses the tree, and returns all the elements with tags that match the String. In this example, it returns all paragraph tags that appear in content. The return value is an Elements object.

Before you go on, you should skim the documentation of these classes so you know what they can do. The most important classes are Element, Elements, and Node, which you can read about at *http://thinkdast.com/jsoupelt*, *http://thinkdast.com/jsoupelts*, and *http://thinkdast.com/jsoupnode*.

Node represents a node in the DOM tree; there are several subclasses that extend Node, including Element, TextNode, DataNode, and Comment. Elements is a Collection of Element objects.

Figure 6-3 is a UML diagram showing the relationships among these classes. In a UML class diagram, a line with a hollow arrowhead indicates that one class extends another. For example, this diagram indicates that Elements extends ArrayList. We'll get back to UML diagrams in "UML Class Diagrams" on page 83.

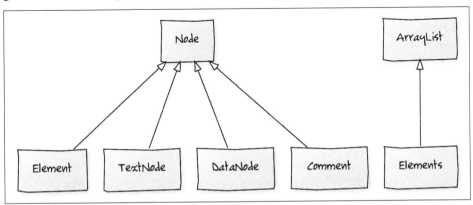

Figure 6-3. UML diagram for selected classes provided by jsoup.

Iterating Through the DOM

To make your life easier, I provide a class called `WikiNodeIterable` that lets you iterate through the nodes in a DOM tree. Here's an example that shows how to use it:

```
Elements paragraphs = content.select("p");
Element firstPara = paragraphs.get(0);

Iterable<Node> iter = new WikiNodeIterable(firstPara);
for (Node node: iter) {
    if (node instanceof TextNode) {
        System.out.print(node);
    }
}
```

This example picks up where the previous one leaves off. It selects the first paragraph in `paragraphs` and then creates a `WikiNodeIterable`, which implements `Iterable<Node>`. `WikiNodeIterable` performs a **depth-first search**, which produces the nodes in the order they would appear on the page.

In this example, we print a `Node` only if it is a `TextNode` and ignore other types of `Node`, specifically the `Element` objects that represent tags. The result is the plain text of the HTML paragraph without any markup. The output is:

Java is a general-purpose computer programming language that is concurrent, class-based, object-oriented,[13] and specifically designed …

Depth-First Search

There are several ways you might reasonably traverse a tree, each with different applications. We'll start with **depth-first search**, or DFS. DFS starts at the root of the tree and selects the first child. If the child has children, it selects the first child again. When it gets to a node with no children, it backtracks, moving up the tree to the parent node, where it selects the next child if there is one; otherwise it backtracks again. When it has explored the last child of the root, it's done.

There are two common ways to implement DFS, recursively and iteratively. The recursive implementation is simple and elegant:

```
private static void recursiveDFS(Node node) {
    if (node instanceof TextNode) {
        System.out.print(node);
    }
    for (Node child: node.childNodes()) {
        recursiveDFS(child);
    }
}
```

This method gets invoked on every Node in the tree, starting with the root. If the Node it gets is a TextNode, it prints the contents. If the Node has any children, it invokes recursiveDFS on each one of them in order.

In this example, we print the contents of each TextNode before traversing the children, so this is an example of a "pre-order" traversal. You can read about "pre-order", "post-order", and "in-order" traversals at *http://thinkdast.com/treetrav*. For this application, the traversal order doesn't matter.

By making recursive calls, recursiveDFS uses the call stack (*http://thinkdast.com/call stack*) to keep track of the child nodes and process them in the right order. As an alternative, we can use a stack data structure to keep track of the nodes ourselves; if we do that, we can avoid the recursion and traverse the tree iteratively.

Stacks in Java

Before I explain the iterative version of DFS, I'll explain the stack data structure. We'll start with the general concept of a stack, which I'll call a "stack" with a lowercase "s". Then we'll talk about two Java interfaces that define stack methods: Stack and Deque.

A stack is a data structure that is similar to a list: it is a collection that maintains the order of the elements. The primary difference between a stack and a list is that the stack provides fewer methods. In the usual convention, it provides:

- push: which adds an element to the top of the stack
- pop: which removes and returns the top-most element from the stack
- peek: which returns the top-most element without modifying the stack
- isEmpty: which indicates whether the stack is empty

Because pop always returns the top-most element, a stack is also called a **LIFO**, which stands for "last in, first out". An alternative to a stack is a **queue**, which returns elements in the same order they are added, that is, "first in, first out", or FIFO.

It might not be obvious why stacks and queues are useful: they don't provide any capabilities that aren't provided by lists; in fact, they provide fewer capabilities. So why not use lists for everything? There are two reasons:

1. If you limit yourself to a small set of methods—that is, a small API—your code will be more readable and less error-prone. For example, if you use a list to represent a stack, you might accidentally remove an element in the wrong order. With the stack API, this kind of mistake is literally impossible. And the best way to avoid errors is to make them impossible.

2. If a data structure provides a small API, it is easier to implement efficiently. For example, a simple way to implement a stack is a singly linked list. When we push an element onto the stack, we add it to the beginning of the list; when we pop an element, we remove it from the beginning. For a linked list, adding and removing from the beginning are constant time operations, so this implementation is efficient. Conversely, big APIs are harder to implement efficiently.

To implement a stack in Java, you have three options:

1. Go ahead and use `ArrayList` or `LinkedList`. If you use `ArrayList`, be sure to add and remove from the *end*, which is a constant time operation. And be careful not to add elements in the wrong place or remove them in the wrong order.

2. Java provides a class called `Stack` that provides the standard set of stack methods. But this class is an old part of Java: it is not consistent with the Java Collections Framework, which came later.

3. Probably the best choice is to use one of the implementations of the `Deque` interface, like `ArrayDeque`.

Deque stands for "double-ended queue"; it's supposed to be pronounced "deck", but some people say "deek". In Java, the `Deque` interface provides push, pop, peek, and isEmpty, so you can use a `Deque` as a stack. It provides other methods, which you can read about at *http://thinkdast.com/deque*, but we won't use them for now.

Iterative DFS

Here is an iterative version of DFS that uses an `ArrayDeque` to represent a stack of Node objects:

```java
private static void iterativeDFS(Node root) {
    Deque<Node> stack = new ArrayDeque<Node>();
    stack.push(root);

    while (!stack.isEmpty()) {
        Node node = stack.pop();
        if (node instanceof TextNode) {
            System.out.print(node);
        }

        List<Node> nodes = new ArrayList<Node>(node.childNodes());
        Collections.reverse(nodes);

        for (Node child: nodes) {
            stack.push(child);
        }
    }
}
```

The parameter, root, is the root of the tree we want to traverse, so we start by creating the stack and pushing the root onto it.

The loop continues until the stack is empty. Each time through, it pops a Node off the stack. If it gets a TextNode, it prints the contents. Then it pushes the children onto the stack. In order to process the children in the right order, we have to push them onto the stack in reverse order; we do that by copying the children into an ArrayList, reversing the elements in place, and then iterating through the reversed ArrayList.

One advantage of the iterative version of DFS is that it is easier to implement as a Java Iterator; you'll see how in the next chapter.

But first, one last note about the Deque interface: in addition to ArrayDeque, Java provides another implementation of Deque, our old friend LinkedList. LinkedList implements both interfaces, List and Deque. Which interface you get depends on how you use it. For example, if you assign a LinkedList object to a Deque variable, like this:

```
Deqeue<Node> deque = new LinkedList<Node>();
```

you can use the methods in the Deque interface, but not all methods in the List interface. If you assign it to a List variable, like this:

```
List<Node> deque = new LinkedList<Node>();
```

you can use List methods but not all Deque methods. And if you assign it like this:

```
LinkedList<Node> deque = new LinkedList<Node>();
```

you can use *all* the methods. But if you combine methods from different interfaces, your code will be less readable and more error-prone.

CHAPTER 7

Getting to Philosophy

The goal of this chapter is to develop a web crawler that tests the "Getting to Philosophy" conjecture, which I presented in "Search Engines" on page 41.

Getting Started

In the repository for this book, you'll find some code to help you get started:

1. `WikiNodeExample.java` contains the code from the previous chapter, demonstrating recursive and iterative implementations of depth-first search (DFS) in a DOM tree.

2. `WikiNodeIterable.java` contains an `Iterable` class for traversing a DOM tree. I'll explain this code in the next section.

3. `WikiFetcher.java` contains a utility class that uses jsoup to download pages from Wikipedia. To help you comply with Wikipedia's terms of service, this class limits how fast you can download pages; if you request more than one page per second, it sleeps before downloading the next page.

4. `WikiPhilosophy.java` contains an outline of the code you will write for this exercise.

You'll also find the Ant build file `build.xml`. If you run `ant WikiPhilosophy`, it will run a simple bit of starter code.

Iterables and Iterators

In the previous chapter, I presented an iterative depth-first search (DFS), and suggested that an advantage of the iterative version, compared to the recursive version, is that it is easier to wrap in an `Iterator` object. In this section we'll see how to do that.

If you are not familiar with the `Iterator` and `Iterable` interfaces, you can read about them at *http://thinkdast.com/iterator* and *http://thinkdast.com/iterable*.

Take a look at the contents of `WikiNodeIterable.java`. The outer class, `WikiNode Iterable` implements the `Iterable<Node>` interface so we can use it in a for loop like this:

```
Node root = ...
Iterable<Node> iter = new WikiNodeIterable(root);
for (Node node: iter) {
    visit(node);
}
```

where `root` is the root of the tree we want to traverse and `visit` is a method that does whatever we want when we "visit" a `Node`.

The implementation of `WikiNodeIterable` follows a conventional formula:

1. The constructor takes and stores a reference to the root `Node`.

2. The `iterator` method creates a returns an `Iterator` object.

Here's what it looks like:

```
public class WikiNodeIterable implements Iterable<Node> {

    private Node root;

    public WikiNodeIterable(Node root) {
        this.root = root;
    }

    @Override
    public Iterator<Node> iterator() {
        return new WikiNodeIterator(root);
    }
}
```

The inner class, `WikiNodeIterator`, does all the real work:

```
private class WikiNodeIterator implements Iterator<Node> {

    Deque<Node> stack;

    public WikiNodeIterator(Node node) {
        stack = new ArrayDeque<Node>();
        stack.push(root);
    }

    @Override
    public boolean hasNext() {
        return !stack.isEmpty();
    }

    @Override
    public Node next() {
        if (stack.isEmpty()) {
            throw new NoSuchElementException();
        }

        Node node = stack.pop();
        List<Node> nodes = new ArrayList<Node>(node.childNodes());
        Collections.reverse(nodes);
        for (Node child: nodes) {
            stack.push(child);
        }
        return node;
    }
}
```

This code is almost identical to the iterative version of DFS, but now it's split into three methods:

1. The constructor initializes the stack (which is implemented using an `ArrayDe` `que`) and pushes the root node onto it.

2. `isEmpty` checks whether the stack is empty.

3. `next` pops the next `Node` off the stack, pushes its children in reverse order, and returns the `Node` it popped. If someone invokes `next` on an empty `Iterator`, it throws an exception.

It might not be obvious that it is worthwhile to rewrite a perfectly good method with two classes and five methods. But now that we've done it, we can use `WikiNodeItera` `ble` anywhere an `Iterable` is called for, which makes it easy and syntactically clean to separate the logic of the iteration (DFS) from whatever processing we are doing on the nodes.

WikiFetcher

When you write a web crawler, it is easy to download too many pages too fast, which might violate the terms of service for the server you are downloading from. To help you avoid that, I provide a class called WikiFetcher that does two things:

1. It encapsulates the code we demonstrated in the previous chapter for downloading pages from Wikipedia, parsing the HTML, and selecting the content text.

2. It measures the time between requests and, if we don't leave enough time between requests, it sleeps until a reasonable interval has elapsed. By default, the interval is one second.

Here's the definition of WikiFetcher:

```java
public class WikiFetcher {
    private long lastRequestTime = -1;
    private long minInterval = 1000;

    /**
     * Fetches and parses a URL string,
     * returning a list of paragraph elements.
     */
    public Elements fetchWikipedia(String url) throws IOException {
        sleepIfNeeded();

        Connection conn = Jsoup.connect(url);
        Document doc = conn.get();
        Element content = doc.getElementById("mw-content-text");
        Elements paragraphs = content.select("p");
        return paragraphs;
    }

    private void sleepIfNeeded() {
        if (lastRequestTime != -1) {
            long currentTime = System.currentTimeMillis();
            long nextRequestTime = lastRequestTime + minInterval;
            if (currentTime < nextRequestTime) {
                try {
                    Thread.sleep(nextRequestTime - currentTime);
                } catch (InterruptedException e) {
                    System.err.println(
                        "Warning: sleep interrupted in fetchWikipedia.");
                }
            }
        }
        lastRequestTime = System.currentTimeMillis();
    }
}
```

The only public method is `fetchWikipedia`, which takes a URL as a `String` and returns an `Elements` collection that contains one DOM element for each paragraph in the content text. This code should look familiar.

The new code is in `sleepIfNeeded`, which checks the time since the last request and sleeps if the elapsed time is less than `minInterval`, which is in milliseconds.

That's all there is to `WikiFetcher`. Here's an example that demonstrates how it's used:

```
WikiFetcher wf = new WikiFetcher();

for (String url: urlList) {
    Elements paragraphs = wf.fetchWikipedia(url);
    processParagraphs(paragraphs);
}
```

In this example, we assume that `urlList` is a collection of `Strings`, and `processPara graphs` is a method that does something with the `Elements` object returned by `fetch Wikipedia`.

This example demonstrates something important: you should create one `Wiki Fetcher` object and use it to handle all requests. If you have multiple instances of `WikiFetcher`, they won't enforce the minimum interval between requests.

NOTE: My implementation of `WikiFetcher` is simple, but it would be easy for someone to misuse it by creating multiple instances. You could avoid this problem by making `WikiFetcher` a **singleton**, which you can read about at *http://thinkdast.com/singleton*.

Exercise 5

In `WikiPhilosophy.java` you'll find a simple `main` method that shows how to use some of these pieces. Starting with this code, your job is to write a crawler that:

1. Takes a URL for a Wikipedia page, downloads it, and parses it.

2. It should traverse the resulting DOM tree to find the first *valid* link. I'll explain what "valid" means below.

3. If the page has no links, or if the first link is a page we have already seen, the program should indicate failure and exit.

4. If the link matches the URL of the Wikipedia page on philosophy, the program should indicate success and exit.

5. Otherwise it should go back to step 1.

The program should build a `List` of the URLs it visits and display the results at the end (whether it succeeds or fails).

So what should we consider a "valid" link? You have some choices here. Various versions of the "Getting to Philosophy" conjecture use slightly different rules, but here are some options:

1. The link should be in the content text of the page, not in a sidebar or boxout.

2. It should not be in italics or in parentheses.

3. You should skip external links, links to the current page, and red links.

4. In some versions, you should skip a link if the text starts with an uppercase letter.

You don't have to enforce all of these rules, but I recommend that you at least handle parentheses, italics, and links to the current page.

If you feel like you have enough information to get started, go ahead. Or you might want to read these hints:

1. As you traverse the tree, the two kinds of Node you will need to deal with are TextNode and Element. If you find an Element, you will probably have to typecast it to access the tag and other information.

2. When you find an Element that contains a link, you can check whether it is in italics by following parent links up the tree. If there is an <i> or <em> tag in the parent chain, the link is in italics.

3. To check whether a link is in parentheses, you will have to scan through the text as you traverse the tree and keep track of opening and closing parentheses (ideally your solution should be able to handle nested parentheses (like this)).

4. If you start from the Java page (*http://thinkdast.com/java*), you should get to "Philosophy" (after following seven links, unless something has changed since I ran the code.

OK, that's all the help you're going to get. Now it's up to you. Have fun!

CHAPTER 8

Indexer

At this point we have built a basic web crawler; the next piece we will work on is the **index**. In the context of web search, an index is a data structure that makes it possible to look up a search term and find the pages where that term appears. In addition, we would like to know how many times the search term appears on each page, which will help identify the pages most relevant to the term.

For example, if a user submits the search terms "Java" and "programming", we would look up both search terms and get two sets of pages. Pages with the word "Java" would include pages about the island of Java, the nickname for coffee, and the programming language. Pages with the word "programming" would include pages about different programming languages, as well as other uses of the word. By selecting pages with both terms, we hope to eliminate irrelevant pages and find the ones about Java programming.

Now that we understand what the index is and what operations it performs, we can design a data structure to represent it.

Data Structure Selection

The fundamental operation of the index is a **lookup**; specifically, we need the ability to look up a term and find all pages that contain it. The simplest implementation would be a collection of pages. Given a search term, we could iterate through the contents of the pages and select the ones that contain the search term. But the runtime would be proportional to the total number of words on all the pages, which would be way too slow.

A better alternative is a **map**, which is a data structure that represents a collection of **key-value pairs** and provides a fast way to look up a **key** and find the corresponding **value**. For example, the first map we'll construct is a TermCounter, which maps from each search term to the number of times it appears in a page. The keys are the search terms and the values are the counts (also called "frequencies").

Java provides an interface called Map that specifies the methods a map should provide; the most important are:

get(key)
    This method looks up a key and returns the corresponding value.

put(key, value)
    This method adds a new key-value pair to the Map, or if the key is already in the map, it replaces the value associated with key.

Java provides several implementations of Map, including the two we will focus on, HashMap and TreeMap. In upcoming chapters, we'll look at these implementations and analyze their performance.

In addition to the TermCounter, which maps from search terms to counts, we will define a class called Index, which maps from a search term to a collection of pages where it appears. And that raises the next question, which is how to represent a collection of pages. Again, if we think about the operations we want to perform, that guides our decision.

In this case, we'll need to combine two or more collections and find the pages that appear in all of them. You might recognize this operation as **set intersection**: the intersection of two sets is the set of elements that appear in both.

As you might expect by now, Java provides a Set interface that defines the operations a set should perform. It doesn't actually provide set intersection, but it provides methods that make it possible to implement intersection and other set operations efficiently. The core Set methods are:

add(element)
    This method adds an element to a set; if the element is already in the set, it has no effect.

contains(element)
    This method checks whether the given element is in the set.

Java provides several implementations of Set, including HashSet and TreeSet.

Now that we've designed our data structures from the top down, we'll implement them from the inside out, starting with TermCounter.

TermCounter

TermCounter is a class that represents a mapping from search terms to the number of times they appear in a page. Here is the first part of the class definition:

```java
public class TermCounter {

    private Map<String, Integer> map;
    private String label;

    public TermCounter(String label) {
        this.label = label;
        this.map = new HashMap<String, Integer>();
    }
}
```

The instance variables are map, which contains the mapping from terms to counts, and label, which identifies the document the terms came from; we'll use it to store URLs.

To implement the mapping, I chose HashMap, which is the most commonly used Map. Coming up in a few chapters, you will see how it works and why it is a common choice.

TermCounter provides put and get, which are defined like this:

```java
public void put(String term, int count) {
    map.put(term, count);
}

public Integer get(String term) {
    Integer count = map.get(term);
    return count == null ? 0 : count;
}
```

put is just a **wrapper method**; when you call put on a TermCounter, it calls put on the embedded map.

On the other hand, get actually does some work. When you call get on a Term Counter, it calls get on the map, and then it checks the result. If the term does not appear in the map, TermCount.get returns 0. Defining get this way makes it easier to write incrementTermCount, which takes a term and increases by one the counter associated with that term:

```java
public void incrementTermCount(String term) {
    put(term, get(term) + 1);
}
```

If the term has not been seen before, get returns 0; we add 1, then use put to add a new key-value pair to the map. If the term is already in the map, we get the old count, add 1, and then store the new count, which replaces the old value.

In addition, `TermCounter` provides these other methods to help with indexing web pages:

```
public void processElements(Elements paragraphs) {
    for (Node node: paragraphs) {
        processTree(node);
    }
}

public void processTree(Node root) {
    for (Node node: new WikiNodeIterable(root)) {
        if (node instanceof TextNode) {
            processText(((TextNode) node).text());
        }
    }
}

public void processText(String text) {
    String[] array = text.replaceAll("\\pP", " ").
                          toLowerCase().
                          split("\\s+");

    for (int i=0; i<array.length; i++) {
        String term = array[i];
        incrementTermCount(term);
    }
}
```

- `processElements` takes an `Elements` object, which is a collection of jsoup `Element` objects. It iterates through the collection and calls `processTree` on each.

- `processTree` takes a jsoup `Node` that represents the root of a DOM tree. It iterates through the tree to find the nodes that contain text; then it extracts the text and passes it to `processText`.

- `processText` takes a `String` that contains words, spaces, punctuation, etc. It removes punctuation characters by replacing them with spaces, converts the remaining letters to lowercase, then splits the text into words. Then it loops through the words it found and calls `incrementTermCount` on each. The `replaceAll` and `split` methods take **regular expressions** as parameters; you can read more about them at *http://thinkdast.com/regex*.

Finally, here's an example that demonstrates how `TermCounter` is used:

```
String url = "http://en.wikipedia.org/wiki/Java_(programming_language)";
WikiFetcher wf = new WikiFetcher();
Elements paragraphs = wf.fetchWikipedia(url);

TermCounter counter = new TermCounter(url);
counter.processElements(paragraphs);
counter.printCounts();
```

This example uses a WikiFetcher to download a page from Wikipedia and parse the main text. Then it creates a TermCounter and uses it to count the words in the page.

In the next section, you'll have a chance to run this code and test your understanding by filling in a missing method.

Exercise 6

In the repository for this book, you'll find the source files for this exercise:

- TermCounter.java contains the code from the previous section.
- TermCounterTest.java contains test code for TermCounter.java.
- Index.java contains the class definition for the next part of this exercise.
- WikiFetcher.java contains the class we used in the previous exercise to download and parse web pages.
- WikiNodeIterable.java contains the class we used to traverse the nodes in a DOM tree.

You'll also find the Ant build file build.xml.

Run ant build to compile the source files. Then run ant TermCounter; it should run the code from the previous section and print a list of terms and their counts. The output should look something like this:

```
genericservlet, 2
configurations, 1
claimed, 1
servletresponse, 2
occur, 2
Total of all counts = -1
```

When you run it, the order of the terms might be different.

The last line is supposed to print the total of the term counts, but it returns -1 because the method size is incomplete. Fill in this method and run ant TermCounter again. The result should be 4798.

Run ant TermCounterTest to confirm that this part of the exercise is complete and correct.

For the second part of the exercise, I'll present an implementation of an Index object and you will fill in a missing method. Here's the beginning of the class definition:

```
public class Index {

    private Map<String, Set<TermCounter>> index =
        new HashMap<String, Set<TermCounter>>();

    public void add(String term, TermCounter tc) {
        Set<TermCounter> set = get(term);

        // if we're seeing a term for the first time, make a new Set
        if (set == null) {
            set = new HashSet<TermCounter>();
            index.put(term, set);
        }
        // otherwise we can modify an existing Set
        set.add(tc);
    }

    public Set<TermCounter> get(String term) {
        return index.get(term);
    }
}
```

The instance variable, index, is a map from each search term to a set of TermCounter objects. Each TermCounter represents a page where the search term appears.

The add method adds a new TermCounter to the set associated with a term. When we index a term that has not appeared before, we have to create a new set. Otherwise we can just add a new element to an existing set. In that case, set.add modifies a set that lives inside index, but doesn't modify index itself. The only time we modify index is when we add a new term.

Finally, the get method takes a search term and returns the corresponding set of Term Counter objects.

This data structure is moderately complicated. To review, an Index contains a Map from each search term to a Set of TermCounter objects, and each TermCounter is a map from search terms to counts.

Figure 8-1 is an object diagram that shows these objects. The Index object has an instance variable named index that refers to a Map. In this example the Map contains only one string, "Java", which maps to a Set that contains two TermCounter objects, one for each page where the word "Java" appears.

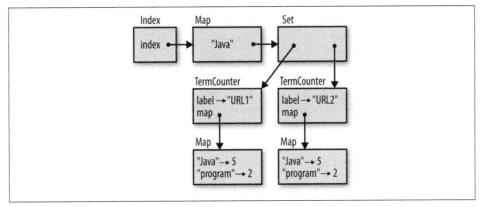

Figure 8-1. Object diagram of an Index.

Each `TermCounter` contains `label`, which is the URL of the page, and `map`, which is a `Map` that contains the words on the page and the number of times each word appears.

The method `printIndex` shows how to unpack this data structure:

```
public void printIndex() {
    // loop through the search terms
    for (String term: keySet()) {
        System.out.println(term);

        // for each term, print pages where it appears and frequencies
        Set<TermCounter> tcs = get(term);
        for (TermCounter tc: tcs) {
            Integer count = tc.get(term);
            System.out.println("    " + tc.getLabel() + " " + count);
        }
    }
}
```

The outer loop iterates the search terms. The inner loop iterates the `TermCounter` objects.

Run `ant build` to make sure your source code is compiled, and then run `ant Index`. It downloads two Wikipedia pages, indexes them, and prints the results; but when you run it you won't see any output because we've left one of the methods empty.

Your job is to fill in `indexPage`, which takes a URL (as a `String`) and an `Elements` object, and updates the index. The following comments sketch what it should do:

```
public void indexPage(String url, Elements paragraphs) {
    // make a TermCounter and count the terms in the paragraphs

    // for each term in the TermCounter, add the TermCounter to the index
}
```

When it's working, run ant `Index` again, and you should see output like this:

```
...
configurations
    http://en.wikipedia.org/wiki/Programming_language 1
    http://en.wikipedia.org/wiki/Java_(programming_language) 1
claimed
    http://en.wikipedia.org/wiki/Java_(programming_language) 1
servletresponse
    http://en.wikipedia.org/wiki/Java_(programming_language) 2
occur
    http://en.wikipedia.org/wiki/Java_(programming_language) 2
```

The order of the search terms might be different when you run it.

Also, run ant `TestIndex` to confirm that this part of the exercise is complete.

CHAPTER 9

The Map Interface

In the next few exercises, I present several implementations of the Map interface. One of them is based on a **hash table**, which is arguably the most magical data structure ever invented. Another, which is similar to TreeMap, is not quite as magical, but it has the added capability that it can iterate the elements in order.

You will have a chance to implement these data structures, and then we will analyze their performance.

But before I can explain hash tables, I'll start with a simple implementation of a Map using a List of key-value pairs.

Implementing MyLinearMap

As usual, I provide starter code and you will fill in the missing methods. Here's the beginning of the MyLinearMap class definition:

```
public class MyLinearMap<K, V> implements Map<K, V> {

    private List<Entry> entries = new ArrayList<Entry>();
```

This class uses two type parameters, K, which is the type of the keys, and V, which is the type of the values. MyLinearMap implements Map, which means it has to provide the methods in the Map interface.

A MyLinearMap object has a single instance variable, entries, which is an ArrayList of Entry objects. Each Entry contains a key-value pair. Here is the definition:

```
public class Entry implements Map.Entry<K, V> {
    private K key;
    private V value;

    public Entry(K key, V value) {
        this.key = key;
        this.value = value;
    }

    @Override
    public K getKey() {
        return key;
    }
    @Override
    public V getValue() {
        return value;
    }
}
```

There's not much to it; an Entry is just a container for a key and a value. This defini-tion is nested inside MyLinearList, so it uses the same type parameters, K and V.

That's all you need to do the exercise, so let's get started.

Exercise 7

In the repository for this book, you'll find the source files for this exercise:

- MyLinearMap.java contains starter code for the first part of the exercise.
- MyLinearMapTest.java contains the unit tests for MyLinearMap.

You'll also find the Ant build file build.xml.

Run ant build to compile the source files. Then run ant MyLinearMapTest; several tests should fail, because you have some work to do!

First, fill in the body of findEntry. This is a helper method that is not part of the Map interface, but once you get it working, you can use it for several methods. Given a target key, it should search through the entries and return the entry that contains the target (as a key, not a value) or null if it's not there. Notice that I have provided an equals method that compares two keys and handles null correctly.

You can run ant MyLinearMapTest again, but even if your findEntry is correct, the tests won't pass because put is not complete.

Fill in put. You should read the documentation of Map.put at *http://thinkdast.com/list put* so you know what it is supposed to do. You might want to start with a version of put that always adds a new entry and does not modify an existing entry; that way you can test the simple case first. Or if you feel more confident, you can write the whole thing at once.

Once you've got put working, the test for containsKey should pass.

Read the documentation of Map.get at *http://thinkdast.com/listget* and then fill in the method. Run the tests again.

Finally, read the documentation of Map.remove at *http://thinkdast.com/maprem* and fill in the method.

At this point, all tests should pass. Congratulations!

Analyzing MyLinearMap

In this section I present a solution to the previous exercise and analyze the performance of the core methods. Here are findEntry and equals:

```
private Entry findEntry(Object target) {
    for (Entry entry: entries) {
        if (equals(target, entry.getKey())) {
            return entry;
        }
    }
    return null;
}

private boolean equals(Object target, Object obj) {
    if (target == null) {
        return obj == null;
    }
    return target.equals(obj);
}
```

The runtime of equals might depend on the size of the target and the keys, but does not generally depend on the number of entries, *n*. So equals is constant time.

In findEntry, we might get lucky and find the key we're looking for at the beginning, but we can't count on it. In general, the number of entries we have to search is proportional to *n*, so findEntry is linear.

Most of the core methods in MyLinearMap use findEntry, including put, get, and remove. Here's what they look like:

```
public V put(K key, V value) {
    Entry entry = findEntry(key);
    if (entry == null) {
        entries.add(new Entry(key, value));
        return null;
    } else {
        V oldValue = entry.getValue();
        entry.setValue(value);
        return oldValue;
    }
}

public V get(Object key) {
    Entry entry = findEntry(key);
    if (entry == null) {
        return null;
    }
    return entry.getValue();
}

public V remove(Object key) {
    Entry entry = findEntry(key);
    if (entry == null) {
        return null;
    } else {
        V value = entry.getValue();
        entries.remove(entry);
        return value;
    }
}
```

After put calls findEntry, everything else is constant time. Remember that entries is an ArrayList, so adding an element *at the end* is constant time, on average. If the key is already in the map, we don't have to add an entry, but we have to call entry.get Value and entry.setValue, and those are both constant time. Putting it all together, put is linear.

By the same reasoning, get is also linear.

remove is slightly more complicated because entries.remove might have to remove an element from the beginning or middle of the ArrayList, and that takes linear time. But that's OK: two linear operations are still linear.

In summary, the core methods are all linear, which is why we called this implementation MyLinearMap (ta-da!).

If we know that the number of entries will be small, this implementation might be good enough, but we can do better. In fact, there is an implementation of Map where all of the core methods are constant time. When you first hear that, it might not seem possible. What I'm saying, in effect, is that you can find a needle in a haystack in constant time, regardless of how big the haystack is. It's magic.

I'll explain how it works in two steps:

1. Instead of storing entries in one big List, we'll break them up into lots of short lists. For each key, we'll use a **hash code** (explained in the next section) to determine which list to use.

2. Using lots of short lists is faster than using just one, but as I'll explain, it doesn't change the order of growth; the core operations are still linear. But there is one more trick: if we increase the number of lists to limit the number of entries per list, the result is a constant-time map. You'll see the details in the next exercise, but first: hashing!

In the next chapter, I'll present a solution, analyze the performance of the core Map methods, and introduce a more efficient implementation.

CHAPTER 10

Hashing

In this chapter, I define `MyBetterMap`, a better implementation of the `Map` interface than `MyLinearMap`, and introduce **hashing**, which makes `MyBetterMap` more efficient.

Hashing

To improve the performance of `MyLinearMap`, we'll write a new class, called `MyBetter Map`, that contains a collection of `MyLinearMap` objects. It divides the keys among the embedded maps, so the number of entries in each map is smaller, which speeds up `findEntry` and the methods that depend on it.

Here's the beginning of the class definition:

```java
public class MyBetterMap<K, V> implements Map<K, V> {

    protected List<MyLinearMap<K, V>> maps;

    public MyBetterMap(int k) {
        makeMaps(k);
    }

    protected void makeMaps(int k) {
        maps = new ArrayList<MyLinearMap<K, V>>(k);
        for (int i=0; i<k; i++) {
            maps.add(new MyLinearMap<K, V>());
        }
    }
}
```

The instance variable, `maps`, is a collection of `MyLinearMap` objects. The constructor takes a parameter, `k`, that determines how many maps to use, at least initially. Then `makeMaps` creates the embedded maps and stores them in an `ArrayList`.

Now, the key to making this work is that we need some way to look at a key and decide which of the embedded maps it should go into. When we put a new key, we choose one of the maps; when we get the same key, we have to remember where we put it.

One possibility is to choose one of the sub-maps at random and keep track of where we put each key. But how should we keep track? It might seem like we could use a Map to look up the key and find the right sub-map, but the whole point of the exercise is to write an efficient implementation of a Map. We can't assume we already have one.

A better approach is to use a **hash function**, which takes an Object, any Object, and returns an integer called a **hash code**. Importantly, if it sees the same Object more than once, it always returns the same hash code. That way, if we use the hash code to store a key, we'll get the same hash code when we look it up.

In Java, every Object provides a method called hashCode that computes a hash function. The implementation of this method is different for different objects; we'll see an example soon.

Here's a helper method that chooses the right sub-map for a given key:

```
protected MyLinearMap<K, V> chooseMap(Object key) {
    int index = 0;
    if (key != null) {
        index = Math.abs(key.hashCode()) % maps.size();
    }
    return maps.get(index);
}
```

If key is null, we choose the sub-map with index 0, arbitrarily. Otherwise we use hashCode to get an integer, apply Math.abs to make sure it is non-negative, then use the remainder operator, %, which guarantees that the result is between 0 and maps.size()-1. So index is always a valid index into maps. Then chooseMap returns a reference to the map it chose.

We use chooseMap in both put and get, so when we look up a key, we get the same map we chose when we added the key. At least, we should—I'll explain a little later why this might not work.

Here's my implementation of put and get:

```
public V put(K key, V value) {
  MyLinearMap<K, V> map = chooseMap(key);
    return map.put(key, value);
}

public V get(Object key) {
    MyLinearMap<K, V> map = chooseMap(key);
    return map.get(key);
}
```

Pretty simple, right? In both methods, we use chooseMap to find the right sub-map and then invoke a method on the sub-map. That's how it works; now let's think about performance.

If there are n entries split up among k sub-maps, there will be n/k entries per map, on average. When we look up a key, we have to compute its hash code, which takes some time, then we search the corresponding sub-map.

Because the entry lists in MyBetterMap are k times shorter than the entry list in MyLinearMap, we expect the search to be k times faster. But the runtime is still proportional to n, so MyBetterMap is still linear. In the next exercise, you'll see how we can fix that.

How Does Hashing Work?

The fundamental requirement for a hash function is that the same object should produce the same hash code every time. For immutable objects, that's relatively easy. For objects with mutable state, we have to think harder.

As an example of an immutable object, we'll define a class called SillyString that encapsulates a String:

```
public class SillyString {
    private final String innerString;

    public SillyString(String innerString) {
        this.innerString = innerString;
    }

    public String toString() {
        return innerString;
    }
```

This class is not very useful, which is why it's called SillyString, but I'll use it to show how a class can define its own hash function:

```
    @Override
    public boolean equals(Object other) {
        return this.toString().equals(other.toString());
    }

    @Override
    public int hashCode() {
        int total = 0;
        for (int i=0; i<innerString.length(); i++) {
            total += innerString.charAt(i);
        }
        return total;
    }
}
```

Notice that SillyString overrides both equals and hashCode. This is important. In order to work properly, equals has to be consistent with hashCode, which means that if two objects are considered equal—that is, equals returns true—they should have the same hash code. But this requirement only works one way; if two objects have the same hash code, they don't necessarily have to be equal.

equals works by invoking toString, which returns innerString. So two Silly String objects are equal if their innerString instance variables are equal.

hashCode works by iterating through the characters in the String and adding them up. When you add a character to an int, Java converts the character to an integer using its Unicode code point. You don't need to know anything about Unicode to understand this example, but if you are curious, you can read more at *http://think dast.com/codepoint*.

This hash function satisfies the requirement: if two SillyString objects contain embedded strings that are equal, they will get the same hash code.

This works correctly, but it might not yield good performance, because it returns the same hash code for many different strings. If two strings contain the same letters in any order, they will have the same hash code. And even if they don't contain the same letters, they might yield the same total, like "ac" and "bb".

If many objects have the same hash code, they end up in the same sub-map. If some sub-maps have more entries than others, the speedup when we have *k* maps might be much less than *k*. So one of the goals of a hash function is to be uniform; that is, it should be equally likely to produce any value in the range. You can read more about designing good hash functions at *http://thinkdast.com/hash*.

Hashing and Mutation

Strings are immutable, and SillyString is also immutable because innerString is declared to be final. Once you create a SillyString, you can't make innerString refer to a different `String`, and you can't modify the `String` it refers to. Therefore, it will always have the same hash code.

But let's see what happens with a mutable object. Here's a definition for `SillyArray`, which is identical to `SillyString`, except that it uses an array of characters instead of a `String`:

```
public class SillyArray {
    private final char[] array;

    public SillyArray(char[] array) {
        this.array = array;
    }

    public String toString() {
        return Arrays.toString(array);
    }

    @Override
    public boolean equals(Object other) {
        return this.toString().equals(other.toString());
    }

    @Override
    public int hashCode() {
        int total = 0;
        for (int i=0; i<array.length; i++) {
            total += array[i];
        }
        System.out.println(total);
        return total;
    }
}
```

`SillyArray` also provides `setChar`, which makes it possible to modify the characters in the array:

```
public void setChar(int i, char c) {
    this.array[i] = c;
}
```

Now suppose we create a `SillyArray` and add it to a map:

```
SillyArray array1 = new SillyArray("Word1".toCharArray());
map.put(array1, 1);
```

The hash code for this array is 461. Now if we modify the contents of the array and then try to look it up, like this:

```
array1.setChar(0, 'C');
Integer value = map.get(array1);
```

the hash code after the mutation is 441. With a different hash code, there's a good chance we'll go looking in the wrong sub-map. In that case, we won't find the key, even though it is in the map. And that's bad.

In general, it is dangerous to use mutable objects as keys in data structures that use hashing, which includes `MyBetterMap` and `HashMap`. If you can guarantee that the keys won't be modified while they are in the map, or that any changes won't affect the hash code, it might be OK. But it is probably a good idea to avoid it.

Exercise 8

In this exercise, you will finish off the implementation of `MyBetterMap`. In the repository for this book, you'll find the source files for this exercise:

- `MyLinearMap.java` contains our solution to the previous exercise, which we will build on in this exercise.
- `MyBetterMap.java` contains the code from the previous chapter with some methods you will fill in.
- `MyHashMap.java` contains the outline of a hash table that grows when needed, which you will complete.
- `MyLinearMapTest.java` contains the unit tests for `MyLinearMap`.
- `MyBetterMapTest.java` contains the unit tests for `MyBetterMap`.
- `MyHashMapTest.java` contains the unit tests for `MyHashMap`.
- `Profiler.java` contains code for measuring and plotting runtime versus problem size.
- `ProfileMapPut.java` contains code that profiles the `Map.put` method.

As usual, you should run `ant build` to compile the source files. Then run `ant MyBetterMapTest`. Several tests should fail, because you have some work to do!

Review the implementation of `put` and `get` from the previous chapter. Then fill in the body of `containsKey`. Hint: Use `chooseMap`. Run `ant MyBetterMapTest` again and confirm that `testContainsKey` passes.

Fill in the body of `containsValue`. Hint: *Don't* use `chooseMap`. Run `ant MyBetterMapTest` again and confirm that `testContainsValue` passes. Notice that we have to do more work to find a value than to find a key.

Like `put` and `get`, this implementation of `containsKey` is linear, because it has to search one of the embedded sub-maps. In the next chapter, we'll see how we can improve this implementation even more.

CHAPTER 11

HashMap

In the previous chapter, we wrote an implementation of the `Map` interface that uses hashing. We expect this version to be faster, because the lists it searches are shorter, but the order of growth is still linear.

If there are n entries and k sub-maps, the size of the sub-maps is n/k on average, which is still proportional to n. But if we increase k along with n, we can limit the size of n/k.

For example, suppose we double k every time n exceeds k; in that case the number of entries per map would be less than 1 on average, and pretty much always less than 10, as long as the hash function spreads out the keys reasonably well.

If the number of entries per sub-map is constant, we can search a single sub-map in constant time. And computing the hash function is generally constant time (it might depend on the size of the key, but does not depend on the number of keys). That makes the core `Map` methods, `put` and `get`, constant time.

In the next exercise, you'll see the details.

Exercise 9

In `MyHashMap.java`, I provide the outline of a hash table that grows when needed. Here's the beginning of the definition:

```
public class MyHashMap<K, V> extends MyBetterMap<K, V> implements Map<K, V> {

    // average number of entries per sub-map before we rehash
    private static final double FACTOR = 1.0;

    @Override
    public V put(K key, V value) {
        V oldValue = super.put(key, value);

        // check if the number of elements per sub-map exceeds the threshold
        if (size() > maps.size() * FACTOR) {
            rehash();
        }
        return oldValue;
    }
}
```

MyHashMap extends MyBetterMap, so it inherits the methods defined there. The only method it overrides is put which calls put in the superclass—that is, it calls the version of put in MyBetterMap—and then checks whether it has to rehash. Calling size returns the total number of entries, n. Calling maps.size returns the number of embedded maps, k.

The constant FACTOR, which is called the **load factor**, determines the maximum number of entries per sub-map, on average. If n > k * FACTOR, that means n/k > FACTOR, which means the number of entries per sub-map exceeds the threshold, so we call rehash.

Run ant build to compile the source files. Then run ant MyHashMapTest. It should fail because the implementation of rehash throws an exception. Your job is to fill it in.

Fill in the body of rehash to collect the entries in the table, resize the table, and then put the entries back in. I provide two methods that might come in handy: MyBetter Map.makeMaps and MyLinearMap.getEntries. Your solution should double the number of maps, k, each time it is called.

Analyzing MyHashMap

If the number of entries in the biggest sub-map is proportional to n/k, and k grows in proportion to n, several of the core MyBetterMap methods become constant time:

```
public boolean containsKey(Object target) {
    MyLinearMap<K, V> map = chooseMap(target);
    return map.containsKey(target);
}

public V get(Object key) {
    MyLinearMap<K, V> map = chooseMap(key);
    return map.get(key);
}

public V remove(Object key) {
    MyLinearMap<K, V> map = chooseMap(key);
    return map.remove(key);
}
```

Each method hashes a key, which is constant time, and then invokes a method on a sub-map, which is constant time.

So far, so good. But the other core method, put, is a little harder to analyze. When we don't have to rehash, it is constant time, but when we do, it's linear. In that way, it's similar to ArrayList.add, which we analyzed in "Classifying add" on page 17.

For the same reason, MyHashMap.put turns out to be constant time if we average over a series of invocations. Again, the argument is based on amortized analysis (see "Classifying add" on page 17).

Suppose the initial number of sub-maps, k, is 2, and the load factor is 1. Now let's see how much work it takes to put a series of keys. As the basic "unit of work", we'll count the number of times we have to hash a key and add it to a sub-map.

The first time we call put it takes 1 unit of work. The second time also takes 1 unit. The third time we have to rehash, so it takes 2 units to rehash the existing keys and 1 unit to hash the new key.

Now the size of the hash table is 4, so the next time we call put, it takes 1 unit of work. But the next time we have to rehash, which takes 4 units to rehash the existing keys and 1 unit to hash the new key.

Figure 11-1 shows the pattern, with the normal work of hashing a new key shown across the bottom and extra work of rehashing shown as a tower.

As the arrows suggest, if we knock down the towers, each one fills the space before the next tower. The result is a uniform height of 2 units, which shows that the average work per put is about 2 units. And that means that put is constant time on average.

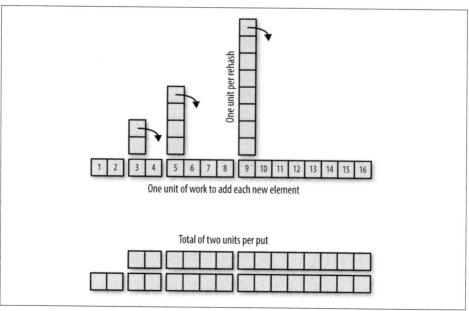

Figure 11-1. Representation of the work done to add elements to a hash table.

This diagram also shows why it is important to double the number of sub-maps, *k*, when we rehash. If we only add to *k* instead of multiplying, the towers would be too close together and they would start piling up. And that would not be constant time.

The Tradeoffs

We've shown that containsKey, get, and remove are constant time, and put is constant time on average. We should take a minute to appreciate how remarkable that is. The performance of these operations is pretty much the same no matter how big the hash table is. Well, sort of.

Remember that our analysis is based on a simple model of computation where each "unit of work" takes the same amount of time. Real computers are more complicated than that. In particular, they are usually fastest when working with data structures small enough to fit in cache; somewhat slower if the structure doesn't fit in cache but still fits in memory; and *much* slower if the structure doesn't fit in memory.

Another limitation of this implementation is that hashing doesn't help if we are given a value rather than a key: containsValue is linear because it has to search all of the sub-maps. And there is no particularly efficient way to look up a value and find the corresponding key (or possibly keys).

And there's one more limitation: some of the methods that were constant time in MyLinearMap have become linear. For example:

```
public void clear() {
    for (int i=0; i<maps.size(); i++) {
        maps.get(i).clear();
    }
}
```

clear has to clear all of the sub-maps, and the number of sub-maps is proportional to
n, so it's linear. Fortunately, this operation is not used very often, so for most applications this tradeoff is acceptable.

Profiling MyHashMap

Before we go on, we should check whether MyHashMap.put is really constant time.

Run ant build to compile the source files. Then run ant ProfileMapPut. It measures the runtime of HashMap.put (provided by Java) with a range of problem sizes, and plots runtime versus problem size on a log-log scale. If this operation is constant time, the total time for n operations should be linear, so the result should be a straight line with slope 1. When I ran this code, the estimated slope was close to 1, which is consistent with our analysis. You should get something similar.

Modify ProfileMapPut.java so it profiles your implementation, MyHashMap, instead of Java's HashMap. Run the profiler again and see if the slope is near 1. You might have to adjust startN and endMillis to find a range of problem sizes where the runtimes are more than a few milliseconds, but not more than a few thousand.

When I ran this code, I got a surprise: the slope was about 1.7, which suggests that this implementation is not constant time after all. It contains a "performance bug".

Before you read the next section, you should track down the error, fix it, and confirm that put is now constant time, as expected.

Fixing MyHashMap

The problem with MyHashMap is in size, which is inherited from MyBetterMap:

```
public int size() {
    int total = 0;
    for (MyLinearMap<K, V> map: maps) {
        total += map.size();
    }
    return total;
}
```

To add up the total size it has to iterate the sub-maps. Since we increase the number of sub-maps, k, as the number of entries, n, increases, k is proportional to n, so size is linear.

And that makes put linear, too, because it uses `size`:

```
public V put(K key, V value) {
    V oldValue = super.put(key, value);

    if (size() > maps.size() * FACTOR) {
        rehash();
    }
    return oldValue;
}
```

Everything we did to make put constant time is wasted if `size` is linear!

Fortunately, there is a simple solution, and we have seen it before: we have to keep the number of entries in an instance variable and update it whenever we call a method that changes it.

You'll find my solution in the repository for this book, in `MyFixedHashMap.java`. Here's the beginning of the class definition:

```
public class MyFixedHashMap<K, V> extends MyHashMap<K, V> implements Map<K, V> {

    private int size = 0;

    public void clear() {
        super.clear();
        size = 0;
    }
```

Rather than modify `MyHashMap`, I define a new class that extends it. It adds a new instance variable, `size`, which is initialized to zero.

Updating `clear` is straightforward; we invoke `clear` in the superclass (which clears the sub-maps), and then update `size`.

Updating `remove` and `put` is a little more difficult because when we invoke the method on the superclass, we can't tell whether the size of the sub-map changed. Here's how I worked around that:

```
public V remove(Object key) {
    MyLinearMap<K, V> map = chooseMap(key);
    size -= map.size();
    V oldValue = map.remove(key);
    size += map.size();
    return oldValue;
}
```

`remove` uses `chooseMap` to find the right sub-map, then subtracts away the size of the sub-map. It invokes `remove` on the sub-map, which may or may not change the size of the sub-map, depending on whether it finds the key. But either way, we add the new size of the sub-map back to `size`, so the final value of `size` is correct.

The rewritten version of put is similar:

```
public V put(K key, V value) {
    MyLinearMap<K, V> map = chooseMap(key);
    size -= map.size();
    V oldValue = map.put(key, value);
    size += map.size();

    if (size() > maps.size() * FACTOR) {
        size = 0;
        rehash();
    }
    return oldValue;
}
```

We have the same problem here: when we invoke put on the sub-map, we don't know whether it added a new entry. So we use the same solution, subtracting off the old size and then adding in the new size.

Now the implementation of the size method is simple:

```
public int size() {
    return size;
}
```

And that's pretty clearly constant time.

When I profiled this solution, I found that the total time for putting n keys is proportional to n, which means that each put is constant time, as it's supposed to be.

UML Class Diagrams

One challenge of working with the code in this chapter is that we have several classes that depend on each other. Here are some of the relationships between the classes:

- MyLinearMap contains a LinkedList and implements Map.
- MyBetterMap contains many MyLinearMap objects and implements Map.
- MyHashMap extends MyBetterMap, so it also contains MyLinearMap objects, and it implements Map.
- MyFixedHashMap extends MyHashMap and implements Map.

To help keep track of relationships like these, software engineers often use **UML class diagrams**. UML stands for Unified Modeling Language (see *http://thinkdast.com/uml*). A **class diagram** is one of several graphical standards defined by UML.

In a class diagram, each class is represented by a box, and relationships between classes are represented by arrows. Figure 11-2 shows a UML class diagram for the classes from the previous exercise, generated using the online tool yUML at *http://yuml.me/*.

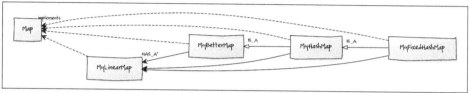

Figure 11-2. UML diagram for the classes in this chapter.

Different relationships are represented by different arrows:

- Arrows with a solid head indicate HAS-A relationships. For example, each instance of `MyBetterMap` contains multiple instances of `MyLinearMap`, so they are connected by a solid arrow.

- Arrows with a hollow head and a solid line indicate IS-A relationships. For example, `MyHashMap` extends `MyBetterMap`, so they are connected by an IS-A arrow.

- Arrows with a hollow head and a dashed line indicate that a class implements an interface; in this diagram, every class implements `Map`.

UML class diagrams provide a concise way to represent a lot of information about a collection of classes. They are used during design phases to communicate about alternative designs, during implementation phases to maintain a shared mental map of the project, and during deployment to document the design.

CHAPTER 12

TreeMap

This chapter presents the binary search tree, which is an efficient implementation of the Map interface that is particularly useful if we want to keep the elements sorted.

What's Wrong with Hashing?

At this point you should be familiar with the Map interface and the HashMap implementation provided by Java. And by making your own Map using a hash table, you should understand how HashMap works and why we expect its core methods to be constant time.

Because of this performance, HashMap is widely used, but it is not the only implementation of Map. There are a few reasons you might want another implementation:

- Hashing can be slow, so even though HashMap operations are constant time, the "constant" might be big.
- Hashing works well if the hash function distributes the keys evenly among the sub-maps. But designing good hash functions is not easy, and if too many keys end up in the same sub-map, the performance of the HashMap may be poor.
- The keys in a hash table are not stored in any particular order; in fact, the order might change when the table grows and the keys are rehashed. For some applications, it is necessary, or at least useful, to keep the keys in order.

It is hard to solve all of these problems at the same time, but Java provides an implementation called TreeMap that comes close:

- It doesn't use a hash function, so it avoids the cost of hashing and the difficulty of choosing a hash function.

- Inside the TreeMap, the keys are are stored in a **binary search tree**, which makes it possible to traverse the keys, in order, in linear time.

- The runtime of the core methods is proportional to log *n*, which is not quite as good as constant time, but is still very good.

In the next section, I'll explain how binary search trees work and then you will use one to implement a Map. Along the way, we'll analyze the performance of the core map methods when implemented using a tree.

Binary Search Tree

A binary search tree (BST) is a tree where each node contains a key, and every node has the "BST property":

1. If node has a left child, all keys in the left subtree must be less than the key in node.

2. If node has a right child, all keys in the right subtree must be greater than the key in node.

Figure 12-1 shows a tree of integers that has this property. This figure is from the Wikipedia page on binary search trees at *http://thinkdast.com/bst*, which you might find useful while you work on this exercise.

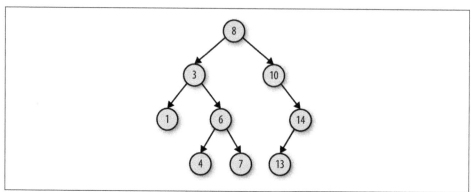

Figure 12-1. Example of a binary search tree.

The key in the root is 8, and you can confirm that all keys to the left of the root are less than 8, and all keys to the right are greater. You can also check that the other nodes have this property.

Looking up a key in a binary search tree is fast because we don't have to search the entire tree. Starting at the root, we can use the following algorithm:

1. Compare the key you are looking for, `target`, to the key in the current node. If they are equal, you are done.

2. If `target` is less than the current key, search the left tree. If there isn't one, `target` is not in the tree.

3. If `target` is greater than the current key, search the right tree. If there isn't one, `target` is not in the tree.

At each level of the tree, you only have to search one child. For example, if you look for `target` = 4 in the previous diagram, you start at the root, which contains the key 8. Because `target` is less than 8, you go left. Because `target` is greater than 3, you go right. Because `target` is less than 6, you go left. And then you find the key you are looking for.

In this example, it takes nine comparisons to find the target, even though the tree contains nine keys. In general, the number of comparisons is proportional to the height of the tree, not the number of keys in the tree.

So what can we say about the relationship between the height of the tree, h, and the number of nodes, n? Starting small and working up:

- If h=1, the tree only contains one node, so n=1.
- If h=2, we can add two more nodes, for a total of n=3.
- If h=3, we can add up to four more nodes, for a total of n=7.
- If h=4, we can add up to eight more nodes, for a total of n=15.

By now you might see the pattern. If we number the levels of the tree from 1 to h, the level with index i can have up to 2^{i-1} nodes. And the total number of nodes in h levels is $2^h - 1$. If we have:

$$n = 2^h - 1$$

we can take the logarithm base 2 of both sides:

$$log_2 n \approx h$$

which means that the height of the tree is proportional to log n, if the tree is full (that is, if each level contains the maximum number of nodes).

So we expect that we can look up a key in a binary search tree in time proportional to log n. This is true if the tree is full, and even if the tree is only partially full. But it is not always true, as we will see.

An algorithm that takes time proportional to log n is called **logarithmic** or **log time**, and it belongs to the order of growth $O(\log n)$.

Exercise 10

For this exercise you will write an implementation of the Map interface using a binary search tree.

Here's the beginning of an implementation, called MyTreeMap:

```
public class MyTreeMap<K, V> implements Map<K, V> {

    private int size = 0;
    private Node root = null;
```

The instance variables are size, which keeps track of the number of keys, and root, which is a reference to the root node in the tree. When the tree is empty, root is null and size is 0.

Here's the definition of Node, which is defined inside MyTreeMap:

```
protected class Node {
    public K key;
    public V value;
    public Node left = null;
    public Node right = null;

    public Node(K key, V value) {
        this.key = key;
        this.value = value;
    }
}
```

Each node contains a key-value pair and references to two child nodes, left and right. Either or both of the child nodes can be null.

Some of the Map methods are easy to implement, like size and clear:

```
public int size() {
    return size;
}

public void clear() {
    size = 0;
    root = null;
}
```

size is clearly constant time.

clear appears to be constant time, but consider this: when root is set to null, the garbage collector reclaims the nodes in the tree, which takes linear time. Should work done by the garbage collector count? I think so.

In the next section, you'll fill in some of the other methods, including the most important ones, get and put.

Implementing a TreeMap

In the repository for this book, you'll find these source files:

- MyTreeMap.java contains the code from the previous section with outlines for the missing methods.
- MyTreeMapTest.java contains the unit tests for MyTreeMap.

Run ant build to compile the source files. Then run ant MyTreeMapTest. Several tests should fail, because you have some work to do!

I've provided outlines for get and containsKey. Both of them use findNode, which is a private method I defined; it is not part of the Map interface. Here's how it starts:

```java
private Node findNode(Object target) {
    if (target == null) {
        throw new IllegalArgumentException();
    }

    @SuppressWarnings("unchecked")
    Comparable<? super K> k = (Comparable<? super K>) target;

    // TODO: FILL THIS IN!
    return null;
}
```

The parameter target is the key we're looking for. If target is null, findNode throws an exception. Some implementations of Map can handle null as a key, but in a binary search tree, we need to be able to compare keys, so dealing with null is problematic. To keep things simple, this implementation does not allow null as a key.

The next lines show how we can compare target to a key in the tree. From the signature of get and containsKey, the compiler considers target to be an Object. But we need to be able to compare keys, so we typecast target to Comparable<? super K>, which means that it is comparable to an instance of type K, or any superclass of K. If you are not familiar with this use of **type wildcards**, you can read more at *http://think dast.com/gentut*.

Fortunately, dealing with Java's type system is not the point of this exercise. Your job is to fill in the rest of findNode. If it finds a node that contains target as a key, it should return the node. Otherwise it should return null. When you get this working, the tests for get and containsKey should pass.

Note that your solution should only search one path through the tree, so it should take time proportional to the height of the tree. You should not search the whole tree!

Your next task is to fill in containsValue. To get you started, I've provided a helper method, equals, that compares target and a given key. Note that the values in the tree (as opposed to the keys) are not necessarily comparable, so we can't use compare To; we have to invoke equals on target.

Unlike your previous solution for findNode, your solution for containsValue *does* have to search the whole tree, so its runtime is proportional to the number of keys, *n*, not the height of the tree, h.

The next method you should fill in is put. I've provided starter code that handles the simple cases:

```
public V put(K key, V value) {
    if (key == null) {
        throw new IllegalArgumentException();
    }
    if (root == null) {
        root = new Node(key, value);
        size++;
        return null;
    }
    return putHelper(root, key, value);
}

private V putHelper(Node node, K key, V value) {
    // TODO: Fill this in.
}
```

If you try to put null as a key, put throws an exception.

If the tree is empty, put creates a new node and initializes the instance variable root.

Otherwise, it calls putHelper, which is a private method I defined; it is not part of the Map interface.

Fill in putHelper so it searches the tree and:

- If key is already in the tree, it replaces the old value with the new, and returns the old value.

- If key is not in the tree, it creates a new node, finds the right place to add it, and returns null.

Your implementation of put should take time proportional to the height of the tree, h, not the number of elements, n. Ideally you should search the tree only once, but if you find it easier to search twice, you can do that; it will be slower, but it doesn't change the order of growth.

Finally, you should fill in the body of keySet. According to the documentation at *http://thinkdast.com/mapkeyset*, this method should return a Set that iterates the keys in order; that is, in increasing order according to the compareTo method. The Hash Set implementation of Set, which we used in "Exercise 6" on page 61, doesn't maintain the order of the keys, but the LinkedHashSet implementation does. You can read about it at *http://thinkdast.com/linkedhashset*.

I've provided an outline of keySet that creates and returns a LinkedHashSet:

```
public Set<K> keySet() {
    Set<K> set = new LinkedHashSet<K>();
    return set;
}
```

You should finish off this method so it adds the keys from the tree to set in ascending order. Hint: You might want to write a helper method; you might want to make it recursive; and you might want to read about in-order tree traversal at *http://think dast.com/inorder*.

When you are done, all tests should pass. In the next chapter, I'll go over my solutions and test the performance of the core methods.

CHAPTER 13

Binary Search Tree

This chapter presents solutions to the previous exercise, then tests the performance of the tree-backed map. I present a problem with the implementation and explain how Java's `TreeMap` solves it.

A Simple MyTreeMap

In the previous exercise I gave you the outline of `MyTreeMap` and asked you to fill in the missing methods. Now I'll present a solution, starting with `findNode`:

```
private Node findNode(Object target) {
    // some implementations can handle null as a key, but not this one
    if (target == null) {
            throw new IllegalArgumentException();
    }

    // something to make the compiler happy
    @SuppressWarnings("unchecked")
    Comparable<? super K> k = (Comparable<? super K>) target;

    // the actual search
    Node node = root;
    while (node != null) {
        int cmp = k.compareTo(node.key);
        if (cmp < 0)
            node = node.left;
        else if (cmp > 0)
            node = node.right;
        else
            return node;
    }
    return null;
}
```

findNode is a private method used by containsKey and get; it is not part of the Map interface. The parameter target is the key we're looking for. I explained the first part of this method in the previous exercise:

- In this implementation, null is not a legal value for a key.

- Before we can invoke compareTo on target, we have to typecast it to some kind of Comparable. The type wildcard used here is as permissive as possible; that is, it works with any type that implements Comparable and whose compareTo method accepts K or any supertype of K.

After all that, the actual search is relatively simple. We initialize a loop variable node so it refers to the root node. Each time through the loop, we compare the target to node.key. If the target is less than the current key, we move to the left child. If it's greater, we move to the right child. And if it's equal, we return the current node.

If we get to the bottom of the tree without finding the target, we conclude that it is not in the tree and return null.

Searching for Values

As I explained in the previous exercise, the runtime of findNode is proportional to the height of the tree, not the number of nodes, because we don't have to search the whole tree. But for containsValue, we have to search the values, not the keys; the BST property doesn't apply to the values, so we have to search the whole tree.

My solution is recursive:

```
public boolean containsValue(Object target) {
    return containsValueHelper(root, target);
}

private boolean containsValueHelper(Node node, Object target) {
    if (node == null) {
        return false;
    }
    if (equals(target, node.value)) {
        return true;
    }
    if (containsValueHelper(node.left, target)) {
        return true;
    }
    if (containsValueHelper(node.right, target)) {
        return true;
    }
    return false;
}
```

`containsValue` takes the target value as a parameter and immediately invokes `con tainsValueHelper`, passing the root of the tree as an additional parameter.

Here's how `containsValueHelper` works:

- The first `if` statement checks the base case of the recursion. If `node` is `null`, that means we have recursed to the bottom of the tree without finding the `target`, so we should return `false`. Note that this only means that the target did not appear on one path through the tree; it is still possible that it will be found on another.

- The second case checks whether we've found what we're looking for. If so, we return `true`. Otherwise, we have to keep going.

- The third case makes a recursive call to search for `target` in the left subtree. If we find it, we can return `true` immediately, without searching the right subtree. Otherwise, we keep going.

- The fourth case searches the right subtree. Again, if we find what we are looking for, we return `true`. Otherwise, having searched the whole tree, we return `false`.

This method visits every node in the tree, so it takes time proportional to the number of nodes.

Implementing put

The `put` method is a little more complicated than `get` because it has to deal with two cases: (1) if the given key is already in the tree, it replaces and returns the old value; (2) otherwise it has to add a new node to the tree, in the right place.

In the previous exercise, I provided this starter code:

```
public V put(K key, V value) {
    if (key == null) {
        throw new IllegalArgumentException();
    }
    if (root == null) {
        root = new Node(key, value);
        size++;
        return null;
    }
    return putHelper(root, key, value);
}
```

and asked you to fill in `putHelper`. Here's my solution:

```
private V putHelper(Node node, K key, V value) {
    Comparable<? super K> k = (Comparable<? super K>) key;
    int cmp = k.compareTo(node.key);

    if (cmp < 0) {
        if (node.left == null) {
            node.left = new Node(key, value);
            size++;
            return null;
        } else {
            return putHelper(node.left, key, value);
        }
    }
    if (cmp > 0) {
        if (node.right == null) {
            node.right = new Node(key, value);
            size++;
            return null;
        } else {
            return putHelper(node.right, key, value);
        }
    }
    V oldValue = node.value;
    node.value = value;
    return oldValue;
}
```

The first parameter, node, is initially the root of the tree, but each time we make a recursive call, it refers to a different subtree. As in get, we use the compareTo method to figure out which path to follow through the tree. If cmp < 0, the key we're adding is less than node.key, so we want to look in the left subtree. There are two cases:

- If the left subtree is empty; that is, if node.left is null, we have reached the bottom of the tree without finding key. At this point, we know that key isn't in the tree, and we know where it should go. So we create a new node and add it as the left child of node.

- Otherwise we make a recursive call to search the left subtree.

If cmp > 0, the key we're adding is greater than node.key, so we want to look in the right subtree. And we handle the same two cases as in the previous branch. Finally, if cmp == 0, we found the key in the tree, so we replace and return the old value.

I wrote this method recursively to make it more readable, but it would be straightforward to rewrite it iteratively, which you might want to do as an exercise.

In-Order Traversal

The last method I asked you to write is keySet, which returns a Set that contains the keys from the tree in ascending order. In other implementations of Map, the keys returned by keySet are in no particular order, but one of the capabilities of the tree implementation is that it is simple and efficient to sort the keys. So we should take advantage of that.

Here's my solution:

```java
public Set<K> keySet() {
    Set<K> set = new LinkedHashSet<K>();
    addInOrder(root, set);
    return set;
}

private void addInOrder(Node node, Set<K> set) {
    if (node == null) return;
    addInOrder(node.left, set);
    set.add(node.key);
    addInOrder(node.right, set);
}
```

In keySet, we create a LinkedHashSet, which is a Set implementation that keeps the elements in order (unlike most other Set implementations). Then we call addInOrder to traverse the tree.

The first parameter, node, is initially the root of the tree, but as you should expect by now, we use it to traverse the tree recursively. addInOrder performs a classic **in-order traversal** of the tree.

If node is null, that means the subtree is empty, so we return without adding anything to set. Otherwise we:

1. Traverse the left subtree in order.
2. Add node.key.
3. Traverse the right subtree in order.

Remember that the BST property guarantees that all nodes in the left subtree are less than node.key, and all nodes in the right subtree are greater. So we know that node.key has been added in the correct order.

Applying the same argument recursively, we know that the elements from the left subtree are in order, as well as the elements from the right subtree. And the base case is correct: if the subtree is empty, no keys are added. So we can conclude that this method adds all keys in the correct order.

Because this method visits every node in the tree, like `containsValue`, it takes time proportional to *n*.

The Logarithmic Methods

In `MyTreeMap`, the methods `get` and `put` take time proportional to the height of the tree, *h*. In the previous exercise, we showed that if the tree is full—if every level of the tree contains the maximum number of nodes—the height of the tree is proportional to log *n*.

And I claimed that `get` and `put` are logarithmic; that is, they take time proportional to log *n*. But for most applications, there's no guarantee that the tree is full. In general, the shape of the tree depends on the keys and what order they are added.

To see how this works out in practice, we'll test our implementation with two sample datasets: a list of random strings and a list of timestamps in increasing order.

Here's the code that generates random strings:

```
Map<String, Integer> map = new MyTreeMap<String, Integer>();

for (int i=0; i<n; i++) {
    String uuid = UUID.randomUUID().toString();
    map.put(uuid, 0);
}
```

`UUID` is a class in the `java.util` package that can generate a random **universally unique identifier**. UUIDs are useful for a variety of applications, but in this example we're taking advantage of an easy way to generate random strings.

I ran this code with n=16384 and measured the runtime and the height of the final tree. Here's the output:

```
Time in milliseconds = 151
Final size of MyTreeMap = 16384
log base 2 of size of MyTreeMap = 14.0
Final height of MyTreeMap = 33
```

I included "log base 2 of size of MyTreeMap" to see how tall the tree would be if it were full. The result indicates that a full tree with height 14 would contain 16,384 nodes.

The actual tree of random strings has height 33, which is substantially more than the theoretical minimum, but not too bad. To find one key in a collection of 16,384, we only have to make 33 comparisons. Compared to a linear search, that's almost 500 times faster.

This performance is typical with random strings or other keys that are added in no particular order. The final height of the tree might be two to three times the theoreti-

---

cal minimum, but it is still proportional to log n, which is much less than n. In fact, log n grows so slowly as n increases, it can be difficult to distinguish logarithmic time from constant time in practice.

However, binary search trees don't always behave so well. Let's see what happens when we add keys in increasing order. Here's an example that measures timestamps in nanoseconds and uses them as keys:

```
MyTreeMap<String, Integer> map = new MyTreeMap<String, Integer>();

for (int i=0; i<n; i++) {
    String timestamp = Long.toString(System.nanoTime());
    map.put(timestamp, 0);
}
```

System.nanoTime returns an integer with type long that indicates elapsed time in nanoseconds. Each time we call it, we get a somewhat bigger number. When we convert these timestamps to strings, they appear in increasing alphabetical order.

And let's see what happens when we run it:

```
Time in milliseconds = 1158
Final size of MyTreeMap = 16384
log base 2 of size of MyTreeMap = 14.0
Final height of MyTreeMap = 16384
```

The runtime is more than seven times longer than in the previous case. longer. If you wonder why, take a look at the final height of the tree: 16,384!

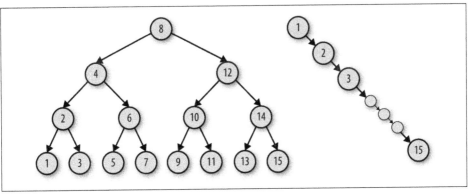

Figure 13-1. Binary search trees, balanced (left) and unbalanced (right).

If you think about how put works, you can figure out what's going on. Every time we add a new key, it's larger than all of the keys in the tree, so we always choose the right subtree, and always add the new node as the right child of the rightmost node. The result is an "unbalanced" tree that only contains right children.

The height of this tree is proportional to *n*, not log *n*, so the performance of get and put is linear, not logarithmic.

Figure 13-1 shows an example of a balanced and unbalanced tree. In the balanced tree, the height is 4 and the total number of nodes is $2^4 - 1 = 15$. In the unbalanced tree with the same number of nodes, the height is 15.

Self-Balancing Trees

There are two possible solutions to this problem:

- You could avoid adding keys to the Map in order. But this is not always possible.
- You could make a tree that does a better job of handling keys if they happen to be in order.

The second solution is better, and there are several ways to do it. The most common is to modify put so that it detects when the tree is starting to become unbalanced and, if so, rearranges the nodes. Trees with this capability are called **self-balancing**. Common self-balancing trees include the AVL tree ("AVL" are the initials of the inventors), and the red-black tree, which is what the Java TreeMap uses.

In our example code, if we replace MyTreeMap with the Java TreeMap, the runtimes are about the same for the random strings and the timestamps. In fact, the timestamps run faster, even though they are in order, probably because they take less time to hash.

In summary, a binary search tree can implement get and put in logarithmic time, but only if the keys are added in an order that keeps the tree sufficiently balanced. Self-balancing trees avoid this problem by doing some additional work each time a new key is added.

You can read more about self-balancing trees at *http://thinkdast.com/balancing*.

One More Exercise

In the previous exercise you didn't have to implement remove, but you might want to try it. If you remove a node from the middle of the tree, you have to rearrange the remaining nodes to restore the BST property. You can probably figure out how to do that on your own, or you can read the explanation at *http://thinkdast.com/bstdel*.

Removing a node and rebalancing a tree are similar operations: if you do this exercise, you will have a better idea of how self-balancing trees work.

CHAPTER 14

Persistence

In the next few exercises we will get back to building a web search engine. To review, the components of a search engine are:

Crawling
> We'll need a program that can download a web page, parse it, and extract the text and any links to other pages.

Indexing
> We'll need an index that makes it possible to look up a search term and find the pages that contain it.

Retrieval
> And we'll need a way to collect results from the index and identify pages that are most relevant to the search terms.

If you did "Exercise 6" on page 61, you implemented an index using Java maps. In this exercise, we'll revisit the indexer and make a new version that stores the results in a database.

If you did "Exercise 5" on page 55, you built a crawler that follows the first link it finds. In the next exercise, we'll make a more general version that stores every link it finds in a queue and explores them in order.

And then, finally, you will work on the retrieval problem.

In these exercises, I provide less starter code, and you will make more design decisions. These exercises are also more open-ended. I will suggest some minimal goals you should try to reach, but there are many ways you can go farther if you want to challenge yourself.

Now, let's get started on a new version of the indexer.

Redis

The previous version of the indexer stores the index in two data structures: a `Term Counter` that maps from a search term to the number of times it appears on a web page, and an `Index` that maps from a search term to the set of pages where it appears.

These data structures are stored in the memory of a running Java program, which means that when the program stops running, the index is lost. Data stored only in the memory of a running program is called **volatile**, because it vaporizes when the program ends.

Data that persists after the program that created it ends is called **persistent**. In general, files stored in a file system are persistent, as well as data stored in databases.

A simple way to make data persistent is to store it in a file. Before the program ends, it could translate its data structures into a format like JSON (*http://thinkdast.com/json*) and then write them into a file. When it starts again, it could read the file and rebuild the data structures.

But there are several problems with this solution:

- Reading and writing large data structures (like a web index) would be slow.
- The entire data structure might not fit into the memory of a single running program.
- If a program ends unexpectedly (for example, due to a power outage), any changes made since the program last started would be lost.

A better alternative is a database that provides persistent storage and the ability to read and write parts of the database without reading and writing the whole thing.

There are many kinds of database management systems (DBMS) that provide different capabilities. You can read an overview at *http://thinkdast.com/database*.

The database I recommend for this exercise is Redis, which provides persistent data structures that are similar to Java data structures. Specifically, it provides:

- Lists of strings, similar to Java `List`
- Hashes, similar to Java `Map`
- Sets of strings, similar to Java `Set`

Redis is a **key-value database**, which means that the data structures it contains (the values) are identified by unique strings (the keys). A key in Redis plays the same role as a reference in Java: it identifies an object. We'll see some examples soon.

Redis Clients and Servers

Redis is usually run as a remote service; in fact, the name stands for "REmote DIctionary Server". To use Redis, you have to run the Redis server somewhere and then connect to it using a Redis client. There are many ways to set up a server and many clients you could use. For this exercise, here is my advice:

- Rather than install and run the server yourself, consider using a service like RedisToGo (*http://thinkdast.com/redistogo*), which runs Redis in the cloud. They offer a free plan with enough resources for the exercise.

- For the client I recommend Jedis, which is a Java library that provides classes and methods for working with Redis.

Here are more detailed instructions to help you get started:

- Create an account on RedisToGo, at *http://thinkdast.com/redissign*, and select the plan you want (probably the free plan to get started).

- Create an **instance**, which is a virtual machine running the Redis server. If you click the "Instances" tab, you should see your new instance, identified by a host name and a port number. For example, I have an instance named "dory-10534".

- Click the instance name to get the configuration page. Make a note of the URL near the top of the page, which looks like this:

      redis://redistogo:1234567feedfacebeefa1e1234567@dory.redistogo.com:10534

This URL contains the server's host name, `dory.redistogo.com`, the port number, `10534`, and the password you will need to connect to the server, which is the long string of letters and numbers in the middle. You will need this information for the next step.

Making a Redis-Backed Index

In the repository for this book, you'll find the source files for this exercise:

- `JedisMaker.java` contains example code for connecting to a Redis server and running a few Jedis methods.

- `JedisIndex.java` contains starter code for this exercise.

- `JedisIndexTest.java` contains test code for `JedisIndex`.

- `WikiFetcher.java` contains the code we saw in previous exercises to read web pages and parse them using jsoup.

You will also need these files, which you worked on in previous exercises:

- `Index.java` implements an index using Java data structures.
- `TermCounter.java` represents a map from terms to their frequencies.
- `WikiNodeIterable.java` iterates through the nodes in a DOM tree produced by jsoup.

If you have working versions of these files, you can use them for this exercise. If you didn't do the previous exercises, or you are not confident in your solutions, you can copy my solutions from the `solutions` folder.

The first step is to use Jedis to connect to your Redis server. `RedisMaker.java` shows how to do this. It reads information about your Redis server from a file, connects to it and logs in using your password, then returns a `Jedis` object you can use to perform Redis operations.

If you open `JedisMaker.java`, you should see the `JedisMaker` class, which is a helper class that provides one static method, `make`, which creates a `Jedis` object. Once this object is authenticated, you can use it to communicate with your Redis database.

`JedisMaker` reads information about your Redis server from a file named `redis_url.txt`, which you should put in the directory `src/resources`:

- Use a text editor to create end edit `ThinkDataStructures/code/src/resources/redis_url.txt`.
- Paste in the URL of your server. If you are using RedisToGo, the URL will look like this:

      redis://redistogo:1234567feedfacebeefa1e1234567@dory.redistogo.com:10534

Because this file contains the password for your Redis server, you should not put this file in a public repository. To help you avoid doing that by accident, the repository contains a `.gitignore` file that makes it harder (but not impossible) to put this file in your repo.

Now run `ant build` to compile the source files and `ant JedisMaker` to run the example code in `main`:

```
public static void main(String[] args) {

    Jedis jedis = make();

    // String
    jedis.set("mykey", "myvalue");
    String value = jedis.get("mykey");
    System.out.println("Got value: " + value);
```

```
// Set
jedis.sadd("myset", "element1", "element2", "element3");
System.out.println("element2 is member: " +
                    jedis.sismember("myset", "element2"));

// List
jedis.rpush("mylist", "element1", "element2", "element3");
System.out.println("element at index 1: " +
                    jedis.lindex("mylist", 1));

// Hash
jedis.hset("myhash", "word1", Integer.toString(2));
jedis.hincrBy("myhash", "word2", 1);
System.out.println("frequency of word1: " +
                    jedis.hget("myhash", "word1"));
System.out.println("frequency of word1: " +
                    jedis.hget("myhash", "word2"));

    jedis.close();
}
```

This example demonstrates the data types and methods you are most likely to use for this exercise. When you run it, the output should be:

```
Got value: myvalue
element2 is member: true
element at index 1: element2
frequency of word1: 2
frequency of word2: 1
```

In the next section, I'll explain how the code works.

Redis Data Types

Redis is basically a map from keys, which are Strings, to values, which can be one of several data types. The most basic Redis data type is a *string*. I will write Redis types in italics to distinguish them from Java types.

To add a *string* to the database, use jedis.set, which is similar to Map.put; the parameters are the new key and the corresponding value. To look up a key and get its value, use jedis.get:

```
jedis.set("mykey", "myvalue");
String value = jedis.get("mykey");
```

In this example, the key is "mykey" and the value is "myvalue".

Redis provides a *set* structure, which is similar to a Java Set<String>. To add elements to a Redis *set*, you choose a key to identify the *set* and then use jedis.sadd:

```
jedis.sadd("myset", "element1", "element2", "element3");
boolean flag = jedis.sismember("myset", "element2");
```

You don't have to create the *set* as a separate step. If it doesn't exist, Redis creates it. In this case, it creates a *set* named myset that contains three elements.

The method jedis.sismember checks whether an element is in a *set*. Adding elements and checking membership are constant time operations.

Redis also provides a *list* structure, which is similar to a Java List<String>. The method jedis.rpush adds elements to the end (right side) of a *list*:

```
jedis.rpush("mylist", "element1", "element2", "element3");
String element = jedis.lindex("mylist", 1);
```

Again, you don't have to create the structure before you start adding elements. This example creates a *list* named "mylist" that contains three elements.

The method jedis.lindex takes an integer index and returns the indicated element of a *list*. Adding and accessing elements are constant time operations.

Finally, Redis provides a *hash* structure, which is similar to a Java Map<String, String>. The method jedis.hset adds a new entry to the *hash*:

```
jedis.hset("myhash", "word1", Integer.toString(2));
String value = jedis.hget("myhash", "word1");
```

This example creates a *hash* named myhash that contains one entry, which maps from the key word1 to the value "2".

The keys and values are *strings*, so if we want to store an Integer, we have to convert it to a String before we call hset. And when we look up the value using hget, the result is a String, so we might have to convert it back to Integer.

Working with Redis *hash*es can be confusing, because we use a key to identify which *hash* we want, and then another key to identify a value in the *hash*. In the context of Redis, the second key is called a **field**, which might help keep things straight. So a "key" like myhash identifies a particular *hash*, and then a "field" like word1 identifies a value in the *hash*.

For many applications, the values in a Redis *hash* are integers, so Redis provides a few special methods, like hincrby, that treat the values as integers:

```
jedis.hincrBy("myhash", "word2", 1);
```

This method accesses myhash, gets the current value associated with word2 (or 0 if it doesn't already exist), increments it by 1, and writes the result back to the *hash*.

Setting, getting, and incrementing entries in a *hash* are constant time operations.

You can read more about Redis data types at *http://thinkdast.com/redistypes*.

Exercise 11

At this point you have the information you need to make a web search index that stores results in a Redis database.

Now run ant `JedisIndexTest`. It should fail, because you have some work to do!

`JedisIndexTest` tests these methods:

- `JedisIndex`, which is the constructor that takes a `Jedis` object as a parameter.
- `indexPage`, which adds a web page to the index; it takes a `String` URL and a jsoup `Elements` object that contains the elements of the page that should be indexed.
- `getCounts`, which takes a search term and returns a `Map<String, Integer>` that maps from each URL that contains the search term to the number of times it appears on that page.

Here's an example of how these methods are used:

```
WikiFetcher wf = new WikiFetcher();
String url1 =
    "http://en.wikipedia.org/wiki/Java_(programming_language)";
Elements paragraphs = wf.readWikipedia(url1);

Jedis jedis = JedisMaker.make();
JedisIndex index = new JedisIndex(jedis);
index.indexPage(url1, paragraphs);
Map<String, Integer> map = index.getCounts("the");
```

If we look up `url1` in the result, `map`, we should get 339, which is the number of times the word "the" appears on the Java Wikipedia page (that is, the version we saved).

If we index the same page again, the new results should replace the old ones.

One suggestion for translating data structures from Java to Redis: remember that each object in a Redis database is identified by a unique key, which is a *string*. If you have two kinds of objects in the same database, you might want to add a prefix to the keys to distinguish between them. For example, in our solution, we have two kinds of objects:

- We define a `URLSet` to be a Redis *set* that contains the URLs that contain a given search term. The key for each `URLSet` starts with `"URLSet:"`, so to get the URLs that contain the word "the", we access the *set* with the key `"URLSet:the"`.

- We define a `TermCounter` to be a Redis *hash* that maps from each term that appears on a page to the number of times it appears. The key for each `Term Counter` starts with `"TermCounter:"` and ends with the URL of the page we're looking up.

In my implementation, there is one `URLSet` for each term and one `TermCounter` for each indexed page. I provide two helper methods, `urlSetKey` and `termCounterKey`, to assemble these keys.

More Suggestions If You Want Them

At this point you have all the information you need to do the exercise, so you can get started if you are ready. But I have a few suggestions you might want to read first:

- For this exercise I provide less guidance than in previous exercises. You will have to make some design decisions; in particular, you will have to figure out how to divide the problem into pieces that you can test one at a time, and then assemble the pieces into a complete solution. If you try to write the whole thing at once, without testing smaller pieces, it might take a very long time to debug.

- One of the challenges of working with persistent data is that it is persistent. The structures stored in the database might change every time you run the program. If you mess something up in the database, you will have to fix it or start over before you can proceed. To help you keep things under control, I've provided methods called `deleteURLSets`, `deleteTermCounters`, and `deleteAllKeys`, which you can use to clean out the database and start fresh. You can also use `printIndex` to print the contents of the index.

- Each time you invoke a `Jedis` method, your client sends a message to the server, then the server performs the action you requested and sends back a message. If you perform many small operations, it will probably take a long time. You can improve performance by grouping a series of operations into a `Transaction`.

For example, here's a simple version of `deleteAllKeys`:

```
public void deleteAllKeys() {
    Set<String> keys = jedis.keys("*");
    for (String key: keys) {
        jedis.del(key);
    }
}
```

Each time you invoke `del` requires a round-trip from the client to the server and back. If the index contains more than a few pages, this method would take a long time to run. We can speed it up with a `Transaction` object:

```
public void deleteAllKeys() {
    Set<String> keys = jedis.keys("*");
    Transaction t = jedis.multi();
    for (String key: keys) {
        t.del(key);
    }
    t.exec();
}
```

`jedis.multi` returns a `Transaction` object, which provides all the methods of a `Jedis` object. But when you invoke a method on a `Transaction`, it doesn't run the operation immediately, and it doesn't communicate with the server. It saves up a batch of operations until you invoke `exec`. Then it sends all of the saved operations to the server at the same time, which is usually much faster.

A Few Design Hints

Now you *really* have all the information you need; you should start working on the exercise. But if you get stuck, or if you really don't know how to get started, you can come back for a few more hints.

Don't read the following until you have run the test code, tried out some basic Redis commands, and written a few methods in `JedisIndex.java`.

OK, if you are really stuck, here are some methods you might want to work on:

```
/**
 * Adds a URL to the set associated with term.
 */
public void add(String term, TermCounter tc) {}

/**
 * Looks up a search term and returns a set of URLs.
 */
public Set<String> getURLs(String term) {}

/**
 * Returns the number of times the given term appears at the given URL.
 */
public Integer getCount(String url, String term) {}

/**
 * Pushes the contents of the TermCounter to Redis.
 */
public List<Object> pushTermCounterToRedis(TermCounter tc) {}
```

These are the methods I used in my solution, but they are certainly not the only way to divide things up. So please take these suggestions if they help, but ignore them if they don't.

For each method, consider writing the tests first. When you figure out how to test a method, you often get ideas about how to write it.

Good luck!

CHAPTER 15

Crawling Wikipedia

In this chapter, I present a solution to the previous exercise and analyze the performance of web indexing algorithms. Then we build a simple web crawler.

The Redis-Backed Indexer

In my solution, we store two kinds of structures in Redis:

- For each search term, we have a URLSet, which is a Redis *set* of URLs that contain the search term.

- For each URL, we have a TermCounter, which is a Redis *hash* that maps each search term to the number of times it appears.

We discussed these data types in the previous chapter. You can also read about Redis structures at *http://thinkdast.com/redistypes*.

In JedisIndex, I provide a method that takes a search term and returns the Redis key of its URLSet:

```
private String urlSetKey(String term) {
    return "URLSet:" + term;
}
```

And a method that takes a URL and returns the Redis key of its TermCounter:

```
private String termCounterKey(String url) {
    return "TermCounter:" + url;
}
```

Here's the implementation of indexPage, which takes a URL and a jsoup Elements object that contains the DOM tree of the paragraphs we want to index:

```
public void indexPage(String url, Elements paragraphs) {
    System.out.println("Indexing " + url);

    // make a TermCounter and count the terms in the paragraphs
    TermCounter tc = new TermCounter(url);
    tc.processElements(paragraphs);

    // push the contents of the TermCounter to Redis
    pushTermCounterToRedis(tc);
}
```

To index a page, we

1. Make a Java TermCounter for the contents of the page, using code from a previous exercise.

2. Push the contents of the TermCounter to Redis.

Here's the new code that pushes a TermCounter to Redis:

```
public List<Object> pushTermCounterToRedis(TermCounter tc) {
    Transaction t = jedis.multi();

    String url = tc.getLabel();
    String hashname = termCounterKey(url);

    // if this page has already been indexed, delete the old hash
    t.del(hashname);

    // for each term, add an entry in the TermCounter and a new
    // member of the index
    for (String term: tc.keySet()) {
        Integer count = tc.get(term);
        t.hset(hashname, term, count.toString());
        t.sadd(urlSetKey(term), url);
    }
    List<Object> res = t.exec();
    return res;
}
```

This method uses a Transaction to collect the operations and send them to the
server all at once, which is much faster than sending a series of small operations.

It loops through the terms in the TermCounter. For each one it

1. Finds or creates a TermCounter on Redis, then adds a field for the new term.

2. Finds or creates a URLSet on Redis, then adds the current URL.

If the page has already been indexed, we delete its old TermCounter before pushing
the new contents.

That's it for indexing new pages.

The second part of the exercise asked you to write `getCounts`, which takes a search term and returns a map from each URL where the term appears to the number of times it appears there. Here is my solution:

```java
public Map<String, Integer> getCounts(String term) {
    Map<String, Integer> map = new HashMap<String, Integer>();
    Set<String> urls = getURLs(term);
    for (String url: urls) {
        Integer count = getCount(url, term);
        map.put(url, count);
    }
    return map;
}
```

This method uses two helper methods:

- `getURLs` takes a search term and returns the Set of URLs where the term appears.

- `getCount` takes a URL and a term and returns the number of times the term appears at the given URL.

Here are the implementations:

```java
public Set<String> getURLs(String term) {
    Set<String> set = jedis.smembers(urlSetKey(term));
    return set;
}

public Integer getCount(String url, String term) {
    String redisKey = termCounterKey(url);
    String count = jedis.hget(redisKey, term);
    return new Integer(count);
}
```

Because of the way we designed the index, these methods are simple and efficient.

Analysis of Lookup

Suppose we have indexed N pages and discovered M unique search terms. How long will it take to look up a search term? Think about your answer before you continue.

To look up a search term, we run `getCounts`, which

1. Creates a map.

2. Runs `getURLs` to get a Set of URLs.

3. For each URL in the Set, runs `getCount` and adds an entry to a `HashMap`.

getURLs takes time proportional to the number of URLs that contain the search term. For rare terms, that might be a small number, but for common terms it might be as large as *N*.

Inside the loop, we run getCount, which finds a TermCounter on Redis, looks up a term, and adds an entry to a HashMap. Those are all constant time operations, so the overall complexity of getCounts is $O(N)$ in the worst case. However, in practice the runtime is proportional to the number of pages that contain the term, which is normally much less than *N*.

This algorithm is as efficient as it can be, in terms of algorithmic complexity, but it is very slow because it sends many small operations to Redis. You can make it faster using a Transaction. You might want to do that as an exercise, or you can see my solution in RedisIndex.java.

Analysis of Indexing

Using the data structures we designed, how long will it take to index a page? Again, think about your answer before you continue.

To index a page, we traverse its DOM tree, find all the TextNode objects, and split up the strings into search terms. That all takes time proportional to the number of words on the page.

For each term, we increment a counter in a HashMap, which is a constant time operation. So making the TermCounter takes time proportional to the number of words on the page.

Pushing the TermCounter to Redis requires deleting a TermCounter, which is linear in the number of unique terms. Then for each term we have to

1. Add an element to a URLSet, and
2. Add an element to a Redis TermCounter.

Both of these are constant time operations, so the total time to push the TermCounter is linear in the number of unique search terms.

In summary, making the TermCounter is proportional to the number of words on the page. Pushing the TermCounter to Redis is proportional to the number of unique terms.

Since the number of words on the page usually exceeds the number of unique search terms, the overall complexity is proportional to the number of words on the page. In theory a page might contain all search terms in the index, so the worst case performance is $O(M)$, but we don't expect to see the worse case in practice.

This analysis suggests a way to improve performance: we should probably avoid indexing very common words. First of all, they take up a lot of time and space, because they appear in almost every URLSet and TermCounter. Furthermore, they are not very useful because they don't help identify relevant pages.

Most search engines avoid indexing common words, which are known in this context as stop words (*http://thinkdast.com/stopword*).

Graph Traversal

If you did the "Getting to Philosophy" exercise in Chapter 7, you already have a program that reads a Wikipedia page, finds the first link, uses the link to load the next page, and repeats. This program is a specialized kind of crawler, but when people say "web crawler" they usually mean a program that

- Loads a starting page and indexes the contents,
- Finds all the links on the page and adds the linked URLs to a collection, and
- Works its way through the collection, loading pages, indexing them, and adding new URLs.
- If it finds a URL that has already been indexed, it skips it.

You can think of the web as a graph where each page is a node and each link is a directed edge from one node to another. If you are not familiar with graphs, you can read about them at *http://thinkdast.com/graph*.

Starting from a source node, a crawler traverses this graph, visiting each reachable node once.

The collection we use to store the URLs determines what kind of traversal the crawler performs:

- If it's a "first in, first out" (FIFO) queue, the crawler performs a breadth-first traversal.
- If it's a "last in, first out" (LIFO) stack, the crawler performs a depth-first traversal.
- More generally, the items in the collection might be prioritized. For example, we might want to give higher priority to pages that have not been indexed for a long time.

You can read more about graph traversal at *http://thinkdast.com/graphtrav*.

Exercise 12

Now it's time to write the crawler. In the repository for this book, you'll find the source files for this exercise:

- WikiCrawler.java, which contains starter code for your crawler
- WikiCrawlerTest.java, which contains test code for WikiCrawler
- JedisIndex.java, which is my solution to the previous exercise

You'll also need some of the helper classes we've used in previous exercises:

- JedisMaker.java
- WikiFetcher.java
- TermCounter.java
- WikiNodeIterable.java

Before you run JedisMaker, you have to provide a file with information about your Redis server. If you did this in the previous exercise, you should be all set. Otherwise you can find instructions in "Making a Redis-Backed Index" on page 103.

Run ant build to compile the source files, then run ant JedisMaker to make sure it is configured to connect to your Redis server.

Now run ant WikiCrawlerTest. It should fail, because you have work to do!

Here's the beginning of the WikiCrawler class I provided:

```
public class WikiCrawler {

    public final String source;
    private JedisIndex index;
    private Queue<String> queue = new LinkedList<String>();
    final static WikiFetcher wf = new WikiFetcher();

    public WikiCrawler(String source, JedisIndex index) {
        this.source = source;
        this.index = index;
        queue.offer(source);
    }

    public int queueSize() {
        return queue.size();
    }
```

We have the following instance variables:

- `source` is the URL where we start crawling.
- `index` is the JedisIndex where the results should go.
- `queue` is a LinkedList where we keep track of URLs that have been discovered but not yet indexed.
- `wf` is the WikiFetcher we'll use to read and parse web pages.

Your job is to fill in `crawl`. Here's the prototype:

```
public String crawl(boolean testing) throws IOException {}
```

The parameter `testing` will be `true` when this method is called from `WikiCrawler Test` and should be `false` otherwise.

When `testing` is `true`, the `crawl` method should:

- Choose and remove a URL from the queue in FIFO order.
- Read the contents of the page using `WikiFetcher.readWikipedia`, which reads cached copies of pages included in this repository for testing purposes (to avoid problems if the Wikipedia version changes).
- Index pages regardless of whether they are already indexed.
- Find all the internal links on the page and add them to the queue in the order they appear. "Internal links" are links to other Wikipedia pages.
- Return the URL of the page it indexed.

When `testing` is `false`, this method should take the following steps:

- Choose and remove a URL from the queue in FIFO order.
- If the URL is already indexed, it should not index it again, and should return `null`.
- Otherwise it should read the contents of the page using `WikiFetcher.fetchWiki pedia`, which reads current content from the web.
- Then it should index the page, add links to the queue, and return the URL of the page it indexed.

`WikiCrawlerTest` loads the queue with about 200 links and then invokes `crawl` three times. After each invocation, it checks the return value and the new length of the queue.

When your crawler is working as specified, this test should pass. Good luck!

CHAPTER 16

Boolean Search

In this chapter I present a solution to the previous exercise. Then you will write code to combine multiple search results and sort them by their relevance to the search terms.

Crawler Solution

First, let's go over our solution to the previous exercise. I provided an outline of Wiki Crawler; your job was to fill in crawl. As a reminder, here are the fields in the Wiki Crawler class:

```java
public class WikiCrawler {
    // keeps track of where we started
    private final String source;

    // the index where the results go
    private JedisIndex index;

    // queue of URLs to be indexed
    private Queue<String> queue = new LinkedList<String>();

    // fetcher used to get pages from Wikipedia
    final static WikiFetcher wf = new WikiFetcher();
}
```

When we create a WikiCrawler, we provide source and index. Initially, queue contains only one element, source.

Notice that the implementation of queue is a LinkedList, so we can add elements at the end—and remove them from the beginning—in constant time. By assigning a LinkedList object to a Queue variable, we limit ourselves to using methods in the

Queue interface; specifically, we'll use `offer` to add elements and `poll` to remove them.

Here's my implementation of `WikiCrawler.crawl`:

```java
public String crawl(boolean testing) throws IOException {
    if (queue.isEmpty()) {
        return null;
    }
    String url = queue.poll();
    System.out.println("Crawling " + url);

    if (testing==false && index.isIndexed(url)) {
        System.out.println("Already indexed.");
        return null;
    }

    Elements paragraphs;
    if (testing) {
        paragraphs = wf.readWikipedia(url);
    } else {
        paragraphs = wf.fetchWikipedia(url);
    }
    index.indexPage(url, paragraphs);
    queueInternalLinks(paragraphs);
    return url;
}
```

Most of the complexity in this method is there to make it easier to test. Here's the logic:

1. If the queue is empty, it returns `null` to indicate that it did not index a page.

2. Otherwise it removes and stores the next URL from the queue.

3. If the URL has already been indexed, `crawl` doesn't index it again, unless it's in testing mode.

4. Next it reads the contents of the page: if it's in testing mode, it reads from a file; otherwise it reads from the web.

5. It indexes the page.

6. It parses the page and adds internal links to the queue.

7. Finally, it returns the URL of the page it indexed.

I presented an implementation of `Index.indexPage` in "The Redis-Backed Indexer" on page 111. So the only new method is `WikiCrawler.queueInternalLinks`.

I wrote two versions of this method with different parameters: one takes an `Elements` object containing one DOM tree per paragraph; the other takes an `Element` object that contains a single paragraph.

The first version just loops through the paragraphs. The second version does the real work:

```
void queueInternalLinks(Elements paragraphs) {
    for (Element paragraph: paragraphs) {
        queueInternalLinks(paragraph);
    }
}

private void queueInternalLinks(Element paragraph) {
    Elements elts = paragraph.select("a[href]");
    for (Element elt: elts) {
        String relURL = elt.attr("href");

        if (relURL.startsWith("/wiki/")) {
            String absURL = elt.attr("abs:href");
            queue.offer(absURL);
        }
    }
}
```

To determine whether a link is "internal," we check whether the URL starts with "/wiki/". This might include some pages we don't want to index, like meta-pages about Wikipedia. And it might exclude some pages we want, like links to pages in non-English languages. But this simple test is good enough to get started.

That's all there is to it. This exercise doesn't have a lot of new material; it is mostly a chance to bring the pieces together.

Information Retrieval

The next phase of this project is to implement a search tool. These are the pieces we'll need:

1. An interface where users can provide search terms and view results

2. A lookup mechanism that takes each search term and returns the pages that contain it

3. Mechanisms for combining search results from multiple search terms

4. Algorithms for ranking and sorting search results

The general term for processes like this is **information retrieval**, which you can read more about at *http://thinkdast.com/infret*.

In this exercise, we'll focus on steps 3 and 4. We've already built a simple version of 2. If you are interested in building web applications, you might consider working on step 1.

Boolean Search

Most search engines can perform **boolean searches**, which means you can combine the results from multiple search terms using boolean logic. For example:

- The search "java AND programming" might return only pages that contain both search terms: "java" and "programming".

- "java OR programming" might return pages that contain either term but not necessarily both.

- "java -indonesia" might return pages that contain "java" and do not contain "indonesia".

Expressions like these that contain search terms and operators are called "queries".

When applied to search results, the boolean operators AND, OR, and - correspond to the set operations intersection, union, and difference. For example, suppose

- s1 is the set of pages containing "java",

- s2 is the set of pages containing "programming", and

- s3 is the set of pages containing "indonesia".

In that case:

- The intersection of s1 and s2 is the set of pages containing "java" AND "programming".

- The union of s1 and s2 is the set of pages containing "java" OR "programming".

- The difference of s1 and s2 is the set of pages containing "java" and not "indonesia".

In the next section you will write a method to implement these operations.

Exercise 13

In the repository for this book you'll find the source files for this exercise:

- WikiSearch.java, which defines an object that contains search results and performs operations on them

- WikiSearchTest.java, which contains test code for WikiSearch

- Card.java, which demonstrates how to use the sort method in java.util.Col lections

You will also find some of the helper classes we've used in previous exercises.

Here's the beginning of the WikiSearch class definition:

```
public class WikiSearch {

    // map from URLs that contain the term(s) to relevance score
    private Map<String, Integer> map;

    public WikiSearch(Map<String, Integer> map) {
        this.map = map;
    }

    public Integer getRelevance(String url) {
        Integer relevance = map.get(url);
        return relevance==null ? 0: relevance;
    }
}
```

A WikiSearch object contains a map from URLs to their relevance score. In the context of information retrieval, a **relevance score** is a number intended to indicate how well a page meets the needs of the user as inferred from the query. There are many ways to construct a relevance score, but most of them are based on **term frequency**, which is the number of times the search terms appear on the page. A common relevance score is called TF-IDF, which stands for "term frequency–inverse document frequency". You can read more about it at *http://thinkdast.com/tfidf*.

You'll have the option to implement TF-IDF later, but we'll start with something even simpler, TF:

- If a query contains a single search term, the relevance of a page is its term frequency; that is, the number of time the term appears on the page.
- For queries with multiple terms, the relevance of a page is the sum of the term frequencies; that is, the total number of times any of the search terms appear.

Now you're ready to start the exercise. Run ant build to compile the source files, then run ant WikiSearchTest. As usual, it should fail, because you have work to do.

In WikiSearch.java, fill in the bodies of and, or, and minus so that the relevant tests pass. You don't have to worry about testSort yet.

You can run WikiSearchTest without using Jedis because it doesn't depend on the index in your Redis database. But if you want to run a query against your index, you have to provide a file with information about your Redis server. See "Making a Redis-Backed Index" on page 103 for details.

Run ant JedisMaker to make sure it is configured to connect to your Redis server. Then run WikiSearch, which prints results from three queries:

- "java"
- "programming"
- "java AND programming"

Initially the results will be in no particular order, because `WikiSearch.sort` is incomplete.

Fill in the body of `sort` so the results are returned in increasing order of relevance. I suggest you use the `sort` method provided by `java.util.Collections`, which sorts any kind of `List`. You can read the documentation at *http://thinkdast.com/collections*.

There are two versions of `sort`:

- The one-parameter version takes a list and sorts the elements using the `compareTo` method, so the elements have to be `Comparable`.
- The two-parameter version takes a list of any object type and a `Comparator`, which is an object that provides a `compare` method that compares elements.

If you are not familiar with the `Comparable` and `Comparator` interfaces, I explain them in the next section.

Comparable and Comparator

The repository for this book includes `Card.java`, which demonstrates two ways to sort a list of `Card` objects. Here's the beginning of the class definition:

```java
public class Card implements Comparable<Card> {

    private final int rank;
    private final int suit;

    public Card(int rank, int suit) {
        this.rank = rank;
        this.suit = suit;
    }
```

A `Card` object has two integer fields, `rank` and `suit`. `Card` implements `Comparable<Card>`, which means that it provides `compareTo`:

```
public int compareTo(Card that) {
    if (this.suit < that.suit) {
        return -1;
    }
    if (this.suit > that.suit) {
        return 1;
    }
    if (this.rank < that.rank) {
        return -1;
    }
    if (this.rank > that.rank) {
        return 1;
    }
    return 0;
}
```

The specification of `compareTo` indicates that it should return a negative number if this is considered less than that, a positive number if it is considered greater, and 0 if they are considered equal.

If you use the one-parameter version of `Collections.sort`, it uses the `compareTo` method provided by the elements to sort them. To demonstrate, we can make a list of 52 cards like this:

```
public static List<Card> makeDeck() {
    List<Card> cards = new ArrayList<Card>();
    for (int suit = 0; suit <= 3; suit++) {
        for (int rank = 1; rank <= 13; rank++) {
            Card card = new Card(rank, suit);
            cards.add(card);
        }
    }
    return cards;
}
```

and sort them like this:

```
Collections.sort(cards);
```

This version of `sort` puts the elements in what's called their "natural order" because it's determined by the objects themselves.

But it is possible to impose a different ordering by providing a `Comparator` object. For example, the natural order of `Card` objects treats Aces as the lowest rank, but in some card games they have the highest rank. We can define a `Comparator` that considers "Aces high", like this:

```
Comparator<Card> comparator = new Comparator<Card>() {
    @Override
    public int compare(Card card1, Card card2) {
        if (card1.getSuit() < card2.getSuit()) {
            return -1;
        }
        if (card1.getSuit() > card2.getSuit()) {
            return 1;
        }
        int rank1 = getRankAceHigh(card1);
        int rank2 = getRankAceHigh(card2);

        if (rank1 < rank2) {
            return -1;
        }
        if (rank1 > rank2) {
            return 1;
        }
        return 0;
    }

    private int getRankAceHigh(Card card) {
        int rank = card.getRank();
        if (rank == 1) {
            return 14;
        } else {
            return rank;
        }
    }
};
```

This code defines an anonymous class that implements compare, as required. Then it creates an instance of the newly defined, unnamed class. If you are not familiar with anonymous classes in Java, you can read about them at *http://thinkdast.com/anon class*.

Using this Comparator, we can invoke sort like this:

```
Collections.sort(cards, comparator);
```

In this ordering, the Ace of Spades is considered the highest class in the deck; the two of Clubs is the lowest.

The code in this section is in Card.java if you want to experiment with it. As an exercise, you might want to write a comparator that sorts by rank first and then by suit, so all the Aces should be together, and all the twos, etc.

Extensions

If you get a basic version of this exercise working, you might want to work on these optional exercises:

- Read about TF-IDF at *http://thinkdast.com/tfidf* and implement it. You might have to modify JavaIndex to compute document frequencies; that is, the total number of times each term appears on all pages in the index.

- For queries with more than one search term, the total relevance for each page is currently the sum of the relevance for each term. Think about when this simple version might not work well, and try out some alternatives.

- Build a user interface that allows users to enter queries with boolean operators. Parse the queries, generate the results, then sort them by relevance and display the highest-scoring URLs. Consider generating snippets that show where the search terms appeared on the page. If you want to make a web application for your user interface, consider using Heroku as a simple option for developing and deploying web applications using Java. See *http://thinkdast.com/heroku*.

CHAPTER 17

Sorting

Computer science departments have an unhealthy obsession with sort algorithms. Based on the amount of time CS students spend on the topic, you would think that choosing sort algorithms is the cornerstone of modern software engineering. Of course, the reality is that software developers can go years, or entire careers, without thinking about how sorting works. For almost all applications, they use whatever general-purpose algorithm is provided by the language or libraries they use. And usually that's just fine.

So if you skip this chapter and learn nothing about sort algorithms, you can still be an excellent developer. But there are a few reasons you might want to do it anyway:

1. Although there are general-purpose algorithms that work well for the vast majority of applications, there are two special-purpose algorithms you might need to know about: radix sort and bounded heap sort.

2. One sort algorithm, merge sort, makes an excellent teaching example because it demonstrates an important and useful strategy for algorithm design, called **divide-conquer-glue**. Also, when we analyze its performance, you will learn about an order of growth we have not seen before, **linearithmic**. Finally, some of the most widely used algorithms are hybrids that include elements of merge sort.

3. One other reason to learn about sort algorithms is that technical interviewers love to ask about them. If you want to get hired, it helps if you can demonstrate CS cultural literacy.

So, in this chapter we'll analyze insertion sort, you will implement merge sort, I'll tell you about radix sort, and you will write a simple version of a bounded heap sort.

Insertion Sort

We'll start with insertion sort, mostly because it is simple to describe and implement. It is not very efficient, but it has some redeeming qualities, as we'll see.

Rather than explain the algorithm here, I suggest you read the insertion sort Wikipedia page at *http://thinkdast.com/insertsort*, which includes pseudocode and animated examples. Come back when you get the general idea.

Here's an implementation of insertion sort in Java:

```
public class ListSorter<T> {

    public void insertionSort(List<T> list, Comparator<T> comparator) {

        for (int i=1; i < list.size(); i++) {
            T elt_i = list.get(i);
            int j = i;
            while (j > 0) {
                T elt_j = list.get(j-1);
                if (comparator.compare(elt_i, elt_j) >= 0) {
                    break;
                }
                list.set(j, elt_j);
                j--;
            }
            list.set(j, elt_i);
        }
    }
}
```

I define a class, `ListSorter`, as a container for sort algorithms. By using the type parameter, T, we can write methods that work on lists containing any object type.

`insertionSort` takes two parameters, a `List` of any kind and a `Comparator` that knows how to compare type T objects. It sorts the list **in place**, which means it modifies the existing list and does not have to allocate any new space.

The following example shows how to call this method with a `List` of `Integer` objects:

```
List<Integer> list = new ArrayList<Integer>(
    Arrays.asList(3, 5, 1, 4, 2));

Comparator<Integer> comparator = new Comparator<Integer>() {
    @Override
    public int compare(Integer elt1, Integer elt2) {
        return elt1.compareTo(elt2);
    }
};
```

```
ListSorter<Integer> sorter = new ListSorter<Integer>();
sorter.insertionSort(list, comparator);
System.out.println(list);
```

`insertionSort` has two nested loops, so you might guess that its runtime is quadratic. In this case, that turns out to be correct, but before you jump to that conclusion, you have to check that the number of times each loop runs is proportional to n, the size of the array.

The outer loop iterates from 1 to `list.size()`, so it is linear in the size of the list, n. The inner loop iterates from i to 0, so it is also linear in n. Therefore, the total number of times the inner loop runs is quadratic.

If you are not sure about that, here's the argument:

- The first time through, $i = 1$ and the inner loop runs at most once.
- The second time, $i = 2$ and the inner loop runs at most twice.
- The last time, $i = n - 1$ and the inner loop runs at most $n - 1$ times.

So the total number of times the inner loop runs is the sum of the series 1, 2, ..., $n - 1$, which is $n(n - 1)/2$. And the leading term of that expression (the one with the highest exponent) is n^2.

In the worst case, insertion sort is quadratic. However:

1. If the elements are already sorted, or nearly so, insertion sort is linear. Specifically, if each element is no more than k locations away from where it should be, the inner loop never runs more than k times, and the total runtime is $O(kn)$.

2. Because the implementation is simple, the overhead is low; that is, although the runtime is an^2, the coefficient of the leading term, a, is probably small.

So if we know that the array is nearly sorted, or is not very big, insertion sort might be a good choice. But for large arrays, we can do better. In fact, much better.

Exercise 14

Merge sort is one of several algorithms whose runtime is better than quadratic. Again, rather than explaining the algorithm here, I suggest you read about it on Wikipedia at *http://thinkdast.com/mergesort*. Once you get the idea, come back and you can test your understanding by writing an implementation.

In the repository for this book, you'll find the source files for this exercise:

- ListSorter.java
- ListSorterTest.java

Run ant build to compile the source files, then run ant ListSorterTest. As usual, it should fail, because you have work to do.

In ListSorter.java, I've provided an outline of two methods, mergeSortInPlace and mergeSort:

```
public void mergeSortInPlace(List<T> list, Comparator<T> comparator) {
    List<T> sorted = mergeSortHelper(list, comparator);
    list.clear();
    list.addAll(sorted);
}

private List<T> mergeSort(List<T> list, Comparator<T> comparator) {
    // TODO: fill this in!
    return null;
}
```

These two methods do the same thing but provide different interfaces. mergeSort takes a list and returns a new list with the same elements sorted in ascending order. mergeSortInPlace is a void method that modifies an existing list.

Your job is to fill in mergeSort. Before you write a fully recursive version of merge sort, start with something like this:

1. Split the list in half.

2. Sort the halves using Collections.sort or insertionSort.

3. Merge the sorted halves into a complete sorted list.

This will give you a chance to debug the merge code without dealing with the complexity of a recursive method.

Next, add a base case (see *http://thinkdast.com/basecase*). If you are given a list with only one element, you could return it immediately, since it is already sorted, sort of. Or if the length of the list is below some threshold, you could sort it using Collections.sort or insertionSort. Test the base case before you proceed.

Finally, modify your solution so it makes two recursive calls to sort the halves of the array. When you get it working, testMergeSort and testMergeSortInPlace should pass.

Analysis of Merge Sort

To classify the runtime of merge sort, it helps to think in terms of levels of recursion and how much work is done on each level. Suppose we start with a list that contains n elements. Here are the steps of the algorithm:

1. Make two new arrays and copy half of the elements into each.

2. Sort the two halves.

3. Merge the halves.

Figure 17-1 shows these steps.

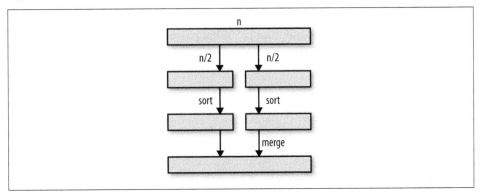

Figure 17-1. Representation of merge sort showing one level of recursion.

The first step copies each of the elements once, so it is linear. The third step also copies each element once, so it is also linear. Now we need to figure out the complexity of step 2. To do that, it helps to looks at a different picture of the computation, which shows the levels of recursion, as in Figure 17-2.

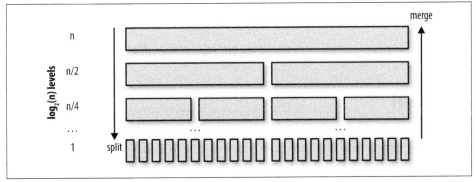

Figure 17-2. Representation of merge sort showing all levels of recursion.

At the top level, we have 1 list with n elements. For simplicity, let's assume n is a power of 2. At the next level there are 2 lists with $n/2$ elements. Then 4 lists with $n/4$ elements, and so on until we get to n lists with 1 element.

On every level we have a total of n elements. On the way down, we have to split the arrays in half, which takes time proportional to n on every level. On the way back up, we have to merge a total of n elements, which is also linear.

If the number of levels is h, the total amount of work for the algorithm is $O(nh)$. So how many levels are there? There are two ways to think about that:

1. How many times do we have to cut n in half to get to 1?
2. Or, how many times do we have to double 1 before we get to n?

Another way to ask the second question is, "What power of 2 is n?"

$$2^h = n$$

Taking the $\log_2$ of both sides yields

$$h = \log_2 n$$

So the total time is $O(n \log n)$. I didn't bother to write the base of the logarithm because logarithms with different bases differ by a constant factor, so all logarithms are in the same order of growth.

Algorithms in $O(n \log n)$ are sometimes called **linearithmic**, but most people just say "n log n".

It turns out that $O(n \log n)$ is the theoretical lower bound for sort algorithms that work by comparing elements to each other. That means there is no **comparison sort** whose order of growth is better than $n \log n$. See *http://thinkdast.com/compsort*.

But as we'll see in the next section, there are non-comparison sorts that take linear time!

Radix Sort

During the 2008 US presidential campaign, candidate Barack Obama was asked to perform an impromptu algorithm analysis when he visited Google. Chief executive Eric Schmidt jokingly asked him for "the most efficient way to sort a million 32-bit integers." Obama had apparently been tipped off, because he quickly replied, "I think the bubble sort would be the wrong way to go." You can watch the video at *http://thinkdast.com/obama*.

Obama was right: bubble sort is conceptually simple but its runtime is quadratic; and even among quadratic sort algorithms, its performance is not very good. See *http://thinkdast.com/bubble*.

The answer Schmidt was probably looking for is "radix sort", which is a **non-comparison** sort algorithm that works if the size of the elements is bounded, like a 32-bit integer or a 20-character string.

To see how this works, imagine you have a stack of index cards where each card contains a three-letter word. Here's how you could sort the cards:

1. Make one pass through the cards and divide them into buckets based on the first letter. So words starting with a should be in one bucket, followed by words starting with b, and so on.

2. Divide each bucket again based on the second letter. So words starting with aa should be together, followed by words starting with ab, and so on. Of course, not all buckets will be full, but that's OK.

3. Divide each bucket again based on the third letter.

At this point each bucket contains one element, and the buckets are sorted in ascending order. Figure 17-3 shows an example with three-letter words.

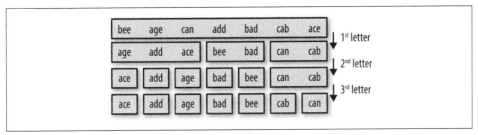

Figure 17-3. Example of radix sort with three-letter words.

The top row shows the unsorted words. The second row shows what the buckets look like after the first pass. The words in each bucket begin with the same letter.

After the second pass, the words in each bucket begin with the same two letters. After the third pass, there can be only one word in each bucket, and the buckets are in order.

During each pass, we iterate through the elements and add them to buckets. As long as the buckets allow addition in constant time, each pass is linear.

The number of passes, which I'll call w, depends on the "width" of the words, but it doesn't depend on the number of words, n. So the order of growth is $O(wn)$, which is linear in n.

There are many variations on radix sort, and many ways to implement each one. You can read more about them at *http://thinkdast.com/radix*. As an optional exercise, consider writing a version of radix sort.

Heap Sort

In addition to radix sort, which applies when the things you want to sort are bounded in size, there is one other special-purpose sorting algorithm you might encounter: **bounded heap sort**. Bounded heap sort is useful if you are working with a very large dataset and you want to report the "Top 10" or "Top k" for some value of *k* much smaller than *n*.

For example, suppose you are monitoring a web service that handles a billion transactions per day. At the end of each day, you want to report the *k* biggest transactions (or slowest, or any other superlative). One option is to store all transactions, sort them at the end of the day, and select the top *k*. That would take time proportional to $n \log n$, and it would be very slow because we probably can't fit a billion transactions in the memory of a single program. We would have to use an "out of core" sort algorithm. You can read about external sorting at *http://thinkdast.com/extsort*.

Using a bounded heap, we can do much better! Here's how we will proceed:

1. I'll explain (unbounded) heap sort.
2. You'll implement it.
3. I'll explain bounded heap sort and analyze it.

To understand heap sort, you have to understand a **heap**, which is a data structure similar to a binary search tree (BST). Here are the differences:

- In a BST, every node, x, has the "BST property": all nodes in the left subtree of x are less than x and all nodes in the right subtree are greater than x.

- In a heap, every node, x, has the "heap property": all nodes in both subtrees of x are greater than x.

- Heaps are like balanced BSTs; when you add or remove elements, they do some extra work to rebalance the tree. As a result, they can be implemented efficiently using an array of elements.

The smallest element in a heap is always at the root, so we can find it in constant time. Adding and removing elements from a heap takes time proportional to the height of the tree *h*. And because the heap is always balanced, *h* is proportional to log *n*. You can read more about heaps at *http://thinkdast.com/heap*.

The Java `PriorityQueue` is implemented using a heap. `PriorityQueue` provides the methods specified in the `Queue` interface, including `offer` and `poll`:

`offer`

Adds an element to the queue, updating the heap so that every node has the "heap property". Takes log n time.

`poll`

Removes the smallest element in the queue from the root and updates the heap. Takes log n time.

Given a `PriorityQueue`, you can easily sort of a collection of n elements like this:

1. Add all elements of the collection to a `PriorityQueue` using `offer`.

2. Remove the elements from the queue using `poll` and add them to a `List`.

Because `poll` returns the smallest element remaining in the queue, the elements are added to the `List` in ascending order. This way of sorting is called **heap sort** (see *http://thinkdast.com/heapsort*).

Adding n elements to the queue takes n log n time. So does removing n elements. So the runtime for heap sort is $O(n \log n)$.

In the repository for this book, in `ListSorter.java` you'll find the outline of a method called `heapSort`. Fill it in and then run `ant ListSorterTest` to confirm that it works.

Bounded Heap

A bounded heap is a heap that is limited to contain at most k elements. If you have n elements, you can keep track of the k largest elements like this:

Initially, the heap is empty. For each element, x:

- Branch 1: If the heap is not full, add x to the heap.

- Branch 2: If the heap is full, compare x to the *smallest* element in the heap. If x is smaller, it cannot be one of the largest k elements, so you can discard it.

- Branch 3: If the heap is full and x is greater than the smallest element in the heap, remove the smallest element from the heap and add x.

Using a heap with the smallest element at the top, we can keep track of the largest k elements. Let's analyze the performance of this algorithm. For each element, we perform one of:

- Branch 1: Adding an element to the heap is $O(\log k)$.

- Branch 2: Finding the smallest element in the heap is $O(1)$.
- Branch 3: Removing the smallest element is $O(\log k)$. Adding x is also $O(\log k)$.

In the worst case, if the elements appear in ascending order, we always run branch 3. In that case, the total time to process n elements is $O(n \log k)$, which is linear in n.

In ListSorter.java you'll find the outline of a method called topK that takes a List, a Comparator, and an integer k. It should return the k largest elements in the List in ascending order. Fill it in and then run ant ListSorterTest to confirm that it works.

Space Complexity

Until now we have talked a lot about runtime analysis, but for many algorithms we are also concerned about space. For example, one of the drawbacks of merge sort is that it makes copies of the data. In our implementation, the total amount of space it allocates is $O(n \log n)$. With a more clever implementation, you can get the space requirement down to $O(n)$.

In contrast, insertion sort doesn't copy the data because it sorts the elements in place. It uses temporary variables to compare two elements at a time, and it uses a few other local variables. But its space use doesn't depend on n.

Our implementation of heap sort creates a new PriorityQueue to store the elements, so the space is $O(n)$; but if you are allowed to sort the list in place, you can run heap sort with $O(1)$ space.

One of the benefits of the bounded heap algorithm you just implemented is that it only needs space proportional to k (the number of elements we want to keep), and k is often much smaller than n.

Software developers tend to pay more attention to runtime than space, and for many applications, that's appropriate. But for large datasets, space can be just as important or more so. For example:

1. If a dataset doesn't fit into the memory of one program, the runtime often increases dramatically, or it might not run at all. If you choose an algorithm that needs less space, and that makes it possible to fit the computation into memory, it might run much faster. In the same vein, a program that uses less space might make better use of CPU caches and run faster (see *http://thinkdast.com/cache*).

2. On a server that runs many programs at the same time, if you can reduce the space needed for each program, you might be able to run more programs on the same server, which reduces hardware and energy costs.

So those are some reasons you should know at least a little bit about the space needs of algorithms.

Index

About the Author

Allen B. Downey is a Professor of Computer Science at Olin College of Engineering. He has taught at Wellesley College, Colby College, and U.C. Berkeley. He has a Ph.D. in Computer Science from U.C. Berkeley and Master's and Bachelor's degrees from MIT.

Colophon

The animal on the cover of *Think Data Structures* is an Australian magpie (*Cracticus tibicen*), a striking black-and-white bird with red eyes. It was called a magpie by European settlers because its plumage was similar to that of the European magpie, but the two species are only distantly related. It is native to Australia and New Guinea.

The Australian magpie is highly intelligent and known for its wide variety of complex calls and birdsong. The birds are generally 14–17 inches long and weigh 7.8–12.3 ounces. They live in a wide range of habitats, including fields, forests, parks, and even residential areas. The magpie is active during the day, and forages on the ground for an omnivorous diet of insects, worms, various invertebrates, nuts, fruit, and small animals like lizards and mice.

In September and October (spring in Australia), male magpies are extremely protective of their nests and chicks, leading to a phenomenon known as "swooping season." The birds aggressively dive at and peck nearby pedestrians and bicyclists, often causing head and face injuries. Some preventative measures include adding fake eyes or long zip ties to a bike helmet, carrying an umbrella, and of course, steering clear of nesting areas entirely. Postal workers are frequent targets of magpie swoops as they travel their routes on motorbikes.

Many of the animals on O'Reilly covers are endangered; all of them are important to the world. To learn more about how you can help, go to *animals.oreilly.com*.

The cover image is from *Lydekker's Royal Natural History*. The cover fonts are URW Typewriter and Guardian Sans. The text font is Adobe Minion Pro; the heading font is Adobe Myriad Condensed; and the code font is Dalton Maag's Ubuntu Mono.

Learn from experts.
Find the answers you need.

Sign up for a **10-day free trial** to get **unlimited access** to all of the content on Safari, including Learning Paths, interactive tutorials, and curated playlists that draw from thousands of ebooks and training videos on a wide range of topics, including data, design, DevOps, management, business—and much more.

Start your free trial at:

oreilly.com/safari

(No credit card required)

Milton Keynes UK
Ingram Content Group UK Ltd.
UKHW030613050124
435493UK00009B/1175

9 781491 972397